Crossway Bible Guide

Series editors: Ian Coffey (NT), Stephen Gaukroger (OT)
Old Testament editor: Stephen Dray

Six minor prophets:
Crossway Bible Guide

Michael Wilcock

Crossway Books Leicester

CROSSWAY BOOKS
38 De Montfort Street, Leicester LE1 7GP, England

First published 1997

British Library Cataloguing in Publication Data

A catalogue record for this book is available from the British Library.

ISBN 1-85684-141-3

Set in Palatino

Typeset in Great Britain by Textype Typesetters, Cambridge

Printed and bound in Great Britain by
The Guernsey Press Co. Ltd., Guernsey, Channel Islands

CONTENTS

Welcome!

These days, meeting together to study the Bible appears to be a booming leisure-time activity in many parts of the world. In the United Kingdom alone, it is estimated that over one million people each week meet in home Bible-study groups.

These Bible Guides have been designed to help such groups and, in particular, those who lead them, but they are eminently suitable for individual study. We are also aware of the needs of those who preach and teach to larger groups as well as the hard-pressed student, all of whom often look for a commentary that gives a concise summary and lively application of a particular passage.

We have therefore enlisted authors who are in the business of teaching the Bible to others and are doing it well. They have kept in their sights two clear aims:

1. To explain and apply the message of the Bible in non-technical language.
2. To encourage discussion, prayer and action on what the Bible teaches.

All of us engaged in the project believe that the Bible is the Word of God – given to us in order that people might discover him and his purposes for our lives. We believe that the sixty-six books which go to make up the Bible, although written by different people, in different places, at different times, through different circumstances, have a single unifying theme: that theme is Salvation. This means free forgiveness and the removal of all our guilt, it means the gift of eternal life and it means the wholeness of purpose and joy which God has designed us to experience here and now, all of this being made possible through the Lord Jesus Christ.

How to use this Bible Guide

These guides have been prepared both for personal study and for the leaders and members of small groups. More information about group study follows on the next few pages.

You can use this book very profitably as a personal study guide. The short studies are ideal for daily reading: the first of the following questions is usually aimed to help you with personal reflection (see *How to tackle personal Bible study*). If you prefer to settle down to a longer period of study you can use three to five studies at a time, and thus get a better overview of a longer Bible passage. In either case using the Bible Guide will help you to be disciplined about regular study, a habit that countless Christians have found greatly beneficial. (See also *How to tackle Six minor prophets* for methods of selecting studies if you do not intend to use them all.)

Yet a third use for these Bible Guides is as a quarry for ideas for the busy Bible teacher, providing outlines and application for those giving talks or sermons or teaching children. You will need more than this book can offer of course, but the way the Bible text is broken down, comments offered and questions raised may well suggest directions to follow.

How to tackle personal Bible study

We have already suggested that you might use this book as a personal study guide. Now for some more detail.

One of the best methods of Bible study is to read the text through carefully several times, possibly using different versions or translations. Having reflected on the material it is a good discipline to write down your own thoughts before doing anything else. At this stage the introduction of other books can be useful. If you are using this book as your main study resource, then read through the relevant sections carefully, turning up the Bible references that are mentioned. The questions at the end of each chapter are specifically designed to help you to apply the passage to your own situation. You may find it helpful to write your answers to the questions in your notes.

It is a good habit to conclude with prayer, bringing before God the things you have learned.

If this kind of in-depth study is too demanding for you and you have only a short time at your disposal, read the Bible passage, read the comments in the Bible Guide, think round one of the questions and commit what you have learned to God in a brief prayer. This would take about fifteen minutes without rushing it.

How to tackle your group Bible study

1. Getting help

If you are new to leading groups you will obviously want to get all the help you can from ministers and experienced friends. Books are also extremely helpful and we strongly recommend a book prepared by the editors of this series of Bible Guides, *Housegroups: the leaders' survival guide*: edited by Ian Coffey and Stephen Gaukroger (Crossway Books, 1996). This book surveys the whole range of different types of group, asking what is the point of it all, what makes a good leader, how to tackle your meeting, how to help the members, how to study, pray, share, worship and plenty of other pointers, tips and guidelines.

This book is a 'must' for all leaders of small groups. It is written by a team of people widely experienced in this area. It is available at your local Christian bookshop. If you have difficulty in obtaining a copy write to Crossway Books, Norton Street, Nottingham, NG7 3HR, UK.

2. Planning your programme with your Bible Guide

This guide is a commentary on God's word, written to help a group to get the most out of their studies. Although it is never ideal to chop up Scripture into small pieces, which the authors never intended, huge chunks are indigestible and we have tried to provide a diet of bite-sized mouthfuls.

If you want to get an overview of the Bible book in a series of meetings you will need to select appropriate studies for each meeting. Read them yourself first and prepare a short summary of the studies you are tackling for your group. Ideally you could write it on a sheet of A5 paper and hand a copy to each member.

Do not attempt to pack more than one study into one meeting but choose the crucial one, the study which best crystallizes the message. There are examples in *How to tackle Six minor prophets* below.

3. Resources

You will find any or all of these books of great value in providing background to your Bible knowledge. Put some of them on your Christmas list and build up your library.

New Bible Dictionary or *New Concise Bible Dictionary* (IVP)
New Bible Atlas (IVP)
New Bible Commentary (21 st Century edition) (IVP)
Everyday Life in Bible Times: John Thompson (IVP)
The Bible User's Manual (IVP)
The Lion Handbook to the Bible (Lion Publishing)
The Message of the Bible (Lion Publishing)
NIV Study Bible (Hodder & Stoughton)
The Bible with pleasure: Stephen Motyer (Crossway Books)

The relevant volume in the IVP Tyndale Commentary series will give you reliable and detailed help with any knotty points you may encounter.

4. Preparing to lead

Reading, discussing with friends, studying, praying, reflecting on life . . . preparation can be endless. But do not be daunted by that. If you wait to become the perfect leader you will never start at all. The really vital elements in preparation are:

▶ prayer (not only in words but an attitude of dependence on God, 'Lord, I can't manage this on my own')

▶ familiarity with the study passage (careful reading of the text, the Bible Guide study and any other resource books that throw light on it) and

▶ a clear idea of where you hope to get in the meeting (notes on your introduction, perhaps, recap what was covered at the last meeting, and what direction you hope the questions will take you in – don't force the group to give your answers).

Here is a short checklist for the busy group leader:

Have I prayed about the meeting?
Have I decided exactly what I want to achieve through the meeting?
Have I prepared the material?
Am I clear about the questions that will encourage positive group discussion?
Am I gently encouraging silent members?
Am I, again gently, quietening the chatterers?
Am I willing to admit ignorance?
Am I willing to listen to what the group says and to value their contributions?
Am I ready not to be dogmatic, not imposing my ideas on the group?
Have I planned how to involve the group in discovering for themselves?
Have I developed several 'prayer points' that will help focus the group?

Are we applying Scripture to our experience of real life or only using it as a peg to hang our opinions on?

Are we finding resources for action and change or just having a nice talk?

Are we all enjoying the experience together?

How to tackle *Six minor prophets*

Now let's assume that you are planning an eight-week course of studies (you will have to make the adjustments if you have more or fewer meetings). Where do you begin? This is entirely up to you and your group of course but, to get you started, here are three possible routes you might take.

1. A bird's eye view

In the opening meeting introduce prophecy and Old Testament prophets in particular; what we expect from them (and must not expect). Invite a minister or other outside speaker. Then take one representative study from each of the six prophets for the next six weeks. On week eight, pool what the group has learned and consider and pray over action to be taken.

2. Interpreting the news headlines

Use the eight studies of the book of Joel to work out your approach to world and local news and how we are to react as Christians to disaster. Look out for the proper balance between formal, gathered worship and private devotion and our picture of God as Lord of creation (1:1–12; 2:21–24); the great judge (1:15; 3:2–16); loving and compassionate (2:12–14); the king who must be honoured (3:17–21).

3. The light and the shadow

We all live with contradictions. Make this point vividly by contrasting emphases. God is both our loving creator and our judge. He calls us to hope and to sober reflection, even fear. Judgment and hope could be used as alternate emphases, for instance:

1. Joel 1:15–20 The Day of the LORD
2. Micah 4:1–8 Hope on the mountain
3. Nahum 3:8–19 'Exterminate!'
4. Micah 4:9–13; 5:1–6 A Shepherd for the flock
5. Habakkuk 1:1–4 A complaint
6. Micah 5:7–15 A preserver for the remnant
7. Zephaniah 2 :1–15 A warning for everyone
8. Micah 7:7–20 Confidence in the incomparable God

These outlines are meant to be springboards for your own ideas, so please do not follow them slavishly. Adapt them for your own use, merge them or ignore them.

What can we expect to learn from these minor prophets?

See pages 17 and 18 for a brief historical introduction, time chart and map. But these prophecies are not mere historical curiosities. Their messages are right up to date for us as we begin a new millennium.

- Joel shows us how to read the news headlines in the light of God's plan for history.

- Obadiah shows us bad people getting their come-uppance, and a lesson to learn from that.

- Micah shows us our incomparable God, and the hope he sets before those who trust and obey him.

- Nahum shows us the proper place for 'righteous anger'.

- Habakkuk shows us how to face the problem of evil.

- Zephaniah shows us the final 'Day of the LORD' – a prospect both alarming and thrilling.

Finding your way round this book

In our Bible Guides we have developed special symbols to make things easier to follow. Every study therefore has an opening section which is the passage in a nutshell.

The main section is the one that *makes sense of the passage*.

Questions

Every passage also has special questions for personal and group study after the main section. Some questions are addressed to us as individuals, some speak to us as members of our church or home group, while others concern us as members of God's people worldwide. The questions are deliberately designed:

▶ to get people thinking about the passage

▶ to apply the text to 'real life' situations

▶ to encourage reflection, discussion and action!

As a group leader you may well discover additional questions that will have special relevance to your group, so look out for these and note them in your preparation time.

Digging deeper

Some passages, however, require an extra amount of explanation, and we have put these sections into two categories. The first kind gives additional background material that helps us to understand something complex. For example, if we dig deeper into the gospels, it helps us to know who the Pharisees were, so that we can see more easily why they related to Jesus in the way they did. These background sections are marked with a spade.

Important doctrines

The second kind of explanatory section appears with passages which have important doctrines contained in them and which we need to study in more depth if we are to grow as Christians. Special sections that explain them to us in greater detail are marked with a face as above.

Some background: when and where

We don't know enough about these six prophets to fit them accurately into a historical time-scale. But broadly speaking they lived during the second half of the period of the Israelite monarchy, the 200-odd years from the late ninth to the early sixth century BC – say from 810 to 580. They brought messages from God mostly to his own people. All six seem to have been based in the southern kingdom of Judah (the northern kingdom, Israel, was destroyed halfway through this period). Messages to God's people then are equally messages to God's people now, however different our circumstances may seem.

The prophetic books of the Old Testament are not arranged in historical order. The chart below gives probable dates:

Prophet	Approx. date (BC)	King(s)	Kingdom
The early, 'non-writing' prophets			
Samuel	1050–1000	Saul, David	United
Elijah	870–852	Ahab, Ahaziah	Israel
Elisha	852–795	Jehoram – Jehoash	Israel
Micaiah	853	Ahab	Israel
The 'writing' prophets of the period of the monarchy			
Joel	810–750	Joash – Uzziah	Judah
Amos	760	Jeroboam II	Israel
Jonah	760	Jeroboam II	Israel
Hosea	760–722	Jeroboam II – Hoshea	Israel
(722 The fall of Samaria)			
Isaiah	740–700	Uzziah – Hezekiah	Judah
Micah	740–687	Jotham – Hezekiah	Judah
Zephaniah	640–610	Josiah	Judah
Nahum	630–612	Josiah – the exile	Judah
Habakkuk	600	Jehoiakim	Judah
(587 The fall of Jerusalem)			
The 'writing' prophets from the period of exile			
Daniel	604–535		
Ezekiel	592–570		
Obadiah	? 587		
Haggai	? 520		
Zechariah	? 520		
Malachi	? 450		

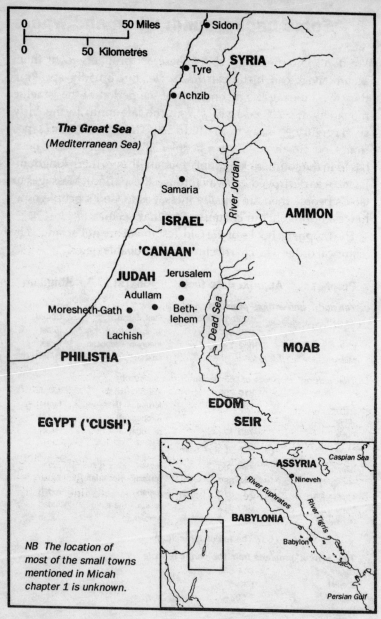

Principal locations mentioned by the Minor Prophets

Introduction

The last twelve books of the Old Testament, generally known as the 'Minor Prophets', are not the easiest or most attractive part of the Bible for modern readers, though if you set out to explore them you will find they contain many a memorable text. But how can we read them as they are meant to be read?

It is untrue to say, as used to be said, that the prophets of the Old Testament were not foretellers, but forthtellers. They were in fact both. They 'told forth' God's message in their own situations, and while their world can seem to us strange and remote, we can usually see equivalent situations in our world to which they have things to say.

They also 'foretold'. Rather than making maps of the future, though, like the countryside as seen by an airman from above, they were exhibiting views, like a traveller's prospect from ground level of what lies before him (though without necessarily explaining how or when he might get there).

In their writings then – six of the twelve 'Minor Prophets' are covered in this book – we shall find God's comments on where we are now, and his explanations of where we are going to, all intended to encourage us to bring our lives into line with his words and ways.

JOEL THE
REPORTER

Joel 1:1-20

Joel 1:1–4

The Lord speaks

This prophecy is supernatural news. It is not to do with the horoscope, though, nor with the 'God-slot', but with today's headlines.

Many of the Old Testament prophets tell us in the introductory words of their books something about who they were and when and where they lived. Joel, however, gives us practically no information of this sort. We soon learn that he is writing against the background of a plague of locusts that has devastated his country, and in due course it appears that that country is Judah. But how all this fits into Judah's history we can only guess.

Ironically, the event which might have fixed a date for Joel is in fact no help at all. The locust-plague was one of the worst in the nation's experience, so bad that at the time you would have thought no-one would ever be able to forget it (verses 2–3). But memories are short. It turned out to be a nine days' wonder, and has not been recorded anywhere in the history books.

Still, at the time it was a catastrophe. Nobody could have been unaffected by it, and everybody, young and old, was called to listen to what God had to say about it. For God intended to use it to teach his people, through his servant Joel, important lessons about himself.

As with every other prophet, these words are not just Joel's but also God's. Joel may be firing the bullets, but God has supplied them. The fact that the book says so little about the prophet himself tells us even more plainly than usual that its real author is the Lord. Like all Old Testament prophecy these chapters are *God speaking*. If, as in most English translations, the message 'came to Joel', it was from God that it came.

How exactly it was conveyed we don't know. The word 'came' might equally be translated 'was' – 'One day there it *was*!' It is almost as though God's message was something that *happened* to Joel.

When the message comes, it is not at first what we might think of as prophecy. It is about neither stars nor souls – that is, in the *Jerusalem Times* it will not be found either in the horoscope or in some religious 'Thought for the Day' column, for it does not predict the future, or talk about 'faith'. Instead, it turns back to page one and hits people with the headlines. It simply makes them look at what is going on around them. God does not want people to ignore the facts and events of their world and to imagine that he is interested only in the world of the 'spirit'. He expects them to be aware of 'the signs of the times' (Matthew 16:3).

Questions

1. What events loom as large in our time as the plague of locusts did in Joel's? If God wants us to take note of such things, what does that tell us about him?
2. We have very little clue as to where Joel fits into Bible history. In what way does this affect our grasp of his message?
3. The handing down of Bible truth from parents to children was taken for granted among God's people in Bible times (verse 3; see Psalm 78:1–8). How much does this happen

today? How could it be encouraged? What if the children won't listen?

Locusts

These insects can cause terrible destruction in the lands of the Middle East. If conditions are right they multiply in uncountable swarms which move across the country devouring every living green thing. The Old Testament has several words for 'locust', and four of them are used in verse 4, giving the effect of successive waves attacking the crops. They may mean something like 'shearer', 'swarmer', 'leaper' and 'destroyer'. A traveller in the Middle East was staying with local people when their community was overwhelmed by a plague of locusts. He wrote afterwards: 'We . . . beat and burned to death heaps upon heaps, but the effort was utterly useless. Wave after wave rolled up the mountains, and poured down upon us, over rocks, walls, ditches and hedges, those behind covering up and bridging over the masses already killed.'

Joel 1:5–14

Don't just sit there

When dreadful things happen and we ask why, are we merely complaining, or do we really want to know?

 Joel is a prophet, but in chapter 1 practically all his 'prophesying' is about the present, not the future. He is calling attention to the events of his own day. This chapter is rather like a newspaper report. Verses 1–3 were the headline: 'Worst In Living Memory!' Verse 4 was the sub-heading: 'Locust devastation hits Israel'. Now in verses 5–14 Joel writes about what has actually happened, and the reactions of various representatives of the public.

He compares the plague of locusts to an invasion by the armies of a powerful foreign nation (verses 6–7), and says the effect on Israel is like that of an untimely bereavement (verse 8). Consumers, the wine-drinkers of verse 5, find themselves deprived of their supplies. Producers, the farmers of verse 11, find that all their labour turns out to be literally fruitless. A reaction is likewise expected from the leaders of the nation, for that is what the priests and elders of verses 13–14 are.

This reporter, however, goes beyond simply recording events, or even how people respond to events. He is one of those journalists who tell people how they *ought* to respond: 'Come on, Israel! Don't just sit there!' There must have been plenty of popular complaining already, but Joel wants to open his readers' eyes to the true grounds for complaint, so that they will see what it is that they should really be deploring.

Without this 'word from the LORD', the consumer society he lives in can see only that Israel is suffering an economic disaster. So to that society he says 'Wake up' (verse 5). They need to see that the reality, and the important thing, is that in this case it is God's own land that has been hurt (verse 6), and God's own house that has been deprived of the offerings that express his people's worship (verses 9, 13). When people are confronted with the evils of the world, there is even today a question which they don't ask nearly often enough: 'How does this offend *God*?'

There is a deeper question too. Certainly, when God's land and God's house are affected by this or that evil, it looks like an attack on God by some enemy of his. Yet at the same time we must wonder how the power of such an enemy and God's own power compare with each other. Surely God is perfectly capable of defending his land and his people against such things? Surely his power is far greater than anyone else's? So if such things do happen, it must be because he has deliberately let them happen. Indeed, if we dare think it, he might even have *made* them happen. And that gives rise to the disturbing question, 'Why would he do that? Has he been provoked into doing it by something *we* have done?'

So we arrive at the place where we see there may be some connection, roundabout but real, between the dreadful things that happen in our society and the things that are not right in ourselves. It recalls the newspaper correspondence on 'What is Wrong with the World', which was effectively ended by a 'letter to the editor' from a certain famous author:

Dear Sir,
    What is wrong with the world?
    I am, Yours faithfully,
    G. K. Chesterton.

When we reach that point we realize why God calls us, through Joel, to confess sin and repent of it (which is the meaning of 'put on sackcloth' in verse 13), and unitedly to 'cry out to the LORD' (verse 14).

Questions

1. What do we learn from these verses about God's power and God's love?
2. In what circumstances today might words like these be addressed to Christians?
3. Does this passage have anything to say about famines in modern times? Is there anything *we* can do about them? Anything we can learn from them?

'God's people'

Through much of Bible history God's people formed a political community, that is, a nation, generally called Israel. In the time of the Judges, they were rather like a federal republic (faintly resembling the United States?). In the time of David and his successors, they were a monarchy. But even in those Old Testament days it was not always so. In the time of Abraham, for example, they were not a nation but simply a family. And it is certainly not so in our New Testament days; ever since the time of Christ, God's people have been, not a nation in the usual sense, but a worldwide fellowship drawn from *all* nations (see Revelation 7:9).

This is one of the respects in which we have to think carefully about how the world of the Old Testament relates to our world. From those Bible times when Israel was a nation, with a government and social institutions and a place in the community of nations, we may well be able to 'read off' lessons for our own secular national life. For at one level there are principles by which Israelite society was meant to live, which are spelt out in the laws of the Old Testament, and from which modern politicians might learn a thing or two if they wanted to govern their own nations well.

But at a deeper level the Israel of Bible times was not just a nation but the people of God, and the only equivalent 'nation' today – the people who have been redeemed by his grace and called by his name – is not the modern state of Israel, nor any other secular nation-state, however much God may seem to have favoured it, but the church of Jesus Christ. So whether or not secular society heeds the message of a book like Joel, the church, which is God's society, is duty bound to find within itself the equivalents of the situations Joel describes, and to take the appropriate action.

Joel 1:15–20

'The day of the LORD'

When 'the day of the Lord' is imminent, the wise thing to do is to call on him.

It is not likely that the 'fire' and 'flames' of verse 19 are to be taken literally. In some parts of the world literal fires, bush fires, are a danger, but Israel does not have the same kind of dense vegetation as those countries. The 'fire' words here are probably picture language not for the plague of locusts itself, but for a drought which seems to have been happening at the same time.

In three ways Joel urges his hearers to turn back to God in repentance and prayer:

▶ The lack of food and water, whether due to locusts or to drought, is described as causing the animals to react as if they were human: they 'groan', they 'are perplexed', they 'are dismayed' (verse 18, RSV), they 'pant for' God (verse 20). If the animals get the point of what is going on, how much more should God's people?

▶ Joel's pronouns become steadily more personal. He has been telling the people that *they* should 'wake up' and repent; now he says, '*We* can see what is happening' (verse 16), and finally comes himself to the place of humble prayer – 'To you, O LORD, *I* call' (verse 19).

▶ He speaks here of 'the day of the LORD' (verse 15). Sometimes God's people understood by that phrase a future event when the Lord would come and put all things to rights by judging and destroying their enemies (for example Isaiah 13:6–11). Sometimes they had to learn that they themselves would come under judgment when that day arrived (for example Amos 5:18). The second point is the one Joel is making here. Either way, the Lord will then be the judge, which is good reason for making sure that we are right with him now. Jesus makes this kind of point in Matthew 5:25.

Joel goes further. The disasters of his own time are not just a pointer towards what 'the day of the LORD' will be like when it eventually arrives (as we might think from the NIV's version, 'it will come', verse 15). They are themselves a 'day of the LORD', which 'is near' – it is coming, it is upon us. It is true that in the New Testament, the 'day of the LORD' is the return of Christ at the end of this age (1 Thessalonians 5:2), and Christ himself has warned us not to imagine that any of the troubles of our own times, however terrible, are necessarily the heralds of that event (Matthew 24:3–8). However, in another sense his 'day' comes again and again to confront his people with its challenge. A nun who was drowned in a shipwreck in 1875 had been heard crying out through the storm, 'Christ, come quickly'. The poet Gerard Manley Hopkins saw that the shipwreck was for her 'the day of the LORD' . That which is '*the cross* to her, she calls *Christ* to her', he says, 'christens her wild-worst Best'.

Questions

1. In what ways ought we to expect 'the day of the LORD' as something imminent?
2. With regard to the final 'Lord's day', how would expectations differ according to whether we were or were not the Lord's people? How can we help people to understand its reality?
3. This is one of the few biblical references to the suffering of animals. Can you think of others? What are we meant to learn from this one?

JOEL THE
LEADER-WRITER

Joel 2:1-27

Joel 2:1–14

Take warning! A terrible mystery

Who is behind the dreadful things that sometimes happen to God's people? Surely not God himself, who is supposed to love them?

In chapter 1 Joel described a shocking event practically as it took place. Now in 2:1–27 (his chapter was originally just these 27 verses) he comments on it. First, like a reporter, he has told us what's happening; now, like a leader-writer, he tells us what's *really* happening!

He takes up three points from his first chapter.

▶ In 2:1–14 he says a great deal more about the plague of locusts and the damage it is causing, reported in 1:4–7. 'This is a trumpet-call to the nation,' he says at the beginning; 'in fact God is speaking to us through it,' he says at the end.

▶ In 2:15–27 he declares that a real spiritual revolution is called for. This half of his 'editorial' also begins with a trumpet-call and ends with a message from God.

▶ In 2:1 and 2:11 he picks up from 1:15 the fact that all this has to do with 'the day of the LORD'.

Take warning

Joel has already reported the arrival of the locusts (1:4). Everyone has seen them. The trumpet-call that begins chapter 2 is a warning, not of their coming, but of what their coming means. The prophet fills out his earlier brief account of the disaster by telling his readers what it *is like*, but he really wants them to grasp what it *is*.

1. He uses a series of metaphors or comparisons to help them see the enormity of what is happening.

▶ The locusts come like the dawn (verse 2). The RSV has 'blackness', translating a different Hebrew word, but whether Joel has in mind the light of morning gradually spreading as day breaks, or the shadows of evening gradually spreading as night falls, the picture is that of the relentless onward march of the locusts across the hills around Jerusalem.

▶ They come like 'a great and powerful people' (verse 2, RSV). There is a whole nation of them, so vast are their numbers.

▶ They come like an army. Joel does not in fact use that word in verse 2, but the next seven verses make this his main picture, and a fearsome one it is.

▶ The picture language tumbles over itself: even while they are like soldiers, they are also like fire burning up stubble (verse 5) and like burglars breaking into houses (verse 9).

2. At the same time Joel is saying not only what the plague is like, but what it really is. It is 'the day of the LORD'. His description begins and ends with this (verses 1–2 and 11), and he doesn't think it any exaggeration to round off his series of pictures with the great cosmic catastrophe of verse 10.

33

A terrible mystery

If the locusts' arrival is 'the day of the LORD,' it opens up a frightening possibility. Does Joel really mean that God himself is bringing about this dreadful event? He seems to be saying so. These destructive hordes are 'his forces', they 'obey his command' (verse 11). It is 'his voice before his army' (RSV) that has ordered the attack. Could he, would he, ever do such evil things?

The question is even more terrible, because it is not just any old god who is acting like this (many of the pagan gods were thought to be quite capable of doing so), but the God of Israel, the LORD, who had promised always to care for his people.

That, though, is the clue to the mystery. For what his voice is actually saying is spelt out in the next three verses (12–14).

▶ He speaks *to his people*: a loving appeal that they should be truly sorry for their sin, and turn away from it and back to him. (Tearing your clothes was an outward sign of grief; something more heartfelt than that was needed.)

▶ He speaks *about himself*: a renewed declaration of the kind of gracious and merciful God he is, as they have known for hundreds of years, ever since he declared it to Moses in Exodus 34:6–7.

Yes, it was his voice that summoned the locusts. He knew it was the only way the people of Joel's time could be made to see where their true welfare lay. Sadly, his people all too often need tough treatment of this kind.

Questions

1. If you look up the word 'evil' in a Bible Concordance, you will see both how much the Lord hates it, and how often he brings it! How do you reconcile these facts?

2. Verse 13 has often been used in Christian worship to call people to the confession of sin. How and why might you find it specially meaningful on such occasions?
3. What relevance would verse 13 have in those parts of the world suffering from hardship like that described by Joel (for example in 1:10, 16–18)?

Joel 2:15–27

Take action! A wonderful promise

God puts right things that go wrong – once we admit it was our fault that they went wrong, and repent.

 After the trumpet-call of 2:1, another one is sounded in 2:15. The first said 'Take warning!' and proclaimed how God punishes sin. The second now says 'Take action!' and calls God's people to repent of their sin. In each case the prophet's words are followed by God's words.

In fact, of course, all the words come from God, and all of them come through the prophet. If it were simply Joel writing down his own idea of what God might have said, we could think of him artfully putting together a kind of poem:

Trumpet 1 (eleven verses);
   God's comment (three verses);
  Trumpet 2 (three verses);
God's comment (ten verses).

But they are God's words, so the poem is his as much as Joel's. He sees to it that they come out the way he wants them, to help his readers grasp and remember his meaning.

Take action

Joel doesn't yet spell out what God's people have to repent of. It could be any sin – your latest sin, or mine. He does spell out what is involved in their repenting, though. If we thought that repentance simply meant saying sorry, we need to think again, especially if it is many of us – a group, a church – who are aware that things are not right between us and God, so that we have together to find the way to real repentance.

Here are a number of things Joel expects when his people turn back to God:

▶ a 'holy fast' (verse 15) – a special occasion of doing without meals (or any other normal, regular activity) to remind themselves that repentance is even more important than such things;

▶ a 'sacred assembly' (verse 15) – God's people coming together in a meeting to encourage one another to get right with him;

▶ a family affair (verse 16) – not one where the old tone down the solemnity of the occasion so as not to bore the young, but one to which children are brought whether or not they understand its gravity;

▶ a 'service' which has worship-leaders and a liturgy (verse 17) – but only so as to put into words what everyone would want to say;

▶ a concentration on the fact that *their* sin is causing *God* to be despised (verse 17). However much trouble his people may cause for themselves when they go their own way, the damage they do to his reputation is a far more serious matter.

A wonderful promise

Verses 18–27 are part of a larger poem (God's comment on Trumpet 2 – see above), but they also form a poem themselves. It has a shape often used by the Old Testament writers, with verses balanced symmetrically round a centre point.

In this case the centre is verse 23. God's promise of rain would be a real answer to prayer if the 'fire' of 1:19 and 2:3 meant that Israel had been suffering from drought as well as locusts. This verse is a pivot:

Israel's Lord (verse 18)
   Satisfaction (verse 19)
      Locusts (verse 20)
         Fruitfulness (verses 21–22)
            God's people rejoice (verse 23)
         Fruitfulness (verse 24)
      Locusts (verse 25)
   Satisfaction (verse 26)
Israel's Lord (verse 27)

The readers of Hebrew poetry found that this sort of structure tended to stick in the mind, just as rhyme and rhythm do in traditional Western poetry.

It is the verses about the locusts that provide us with a small puzzle and a great promise.

► The puzzle of verse 20 is the word 'northern'. Probably the meaning is that the locusts, like so many of Israel's invaders, had come down from the north. Perhaps it was a wind from God from the same direction which also eventually drove them on out of Israelite territory, some down into the southern desert, some into the Dead Sea, and some into the Mediterranean.

► The promise of verse 25 is one of the most memorable promises in the Bible. God's people have often found themselves in situations like this, when years of labour seem to go for nothing, and there is no fruit to show for them. But God is the great Restorer of things that are spoiled, and he does restore the years that the locust has eaten (see the RSV). And if we were to say, 'But this time it was my own fault, and I don't deserve to have the loss made up to me', it would be precisely for us that this promise would be intended! That is what makes it so wonderful. It is a promise of *grace*, that is, of *undeserved* mercy.

Questions

1. How and when might a 'sacred assembly' like that of 2:15–17 be called together in today's church? How could everybody take an active part in it?
2. Even in the 'restoration' verse God is still insisting that the locusts were 'my great army, that I sent among you' (verse 25). How do his roles as both Restorer and Punisher fit together?
3. Could you ever be sure nowadays that famine (or plenty) was a sign of God's displeasure (or mercy)? Does God reward his servants with riches and punish sinners with poverty? How can we explain these problems to ourselves and to unbelievers?

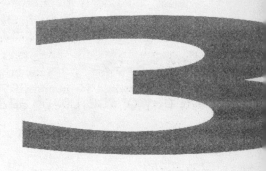

JOEL THE
FORECASTER

Joel 2:28 – 3:21

Joel 2:28–32

'The day of the LORD' again

Another, very special, day of the LORD was on its way. For us it has arrived. What Joel saw as a far-off promise has now come true for God's people.

Joel's 'front page' carried the disaster headlines, and turning the pages we then came to his editorial comment. Now he gives us something different. Towards the back of many newspapers you find horoscopes, in which (unlike the journalists who tell us what has happened and what is happening) resident stargazers describe, for those who are foolish enough to believe them, what is supposedly going to happen in the future.

What the stars are supposed to foretell is, of course, all nonsense. Joel sees a time coming when the stars will in any case no longer shine (3:15)! But he, being a prophet of God, really can foretell the future, and here in 2:28–32 (which originally, in the Hebrew Bible, formed a separate chapter just five verses long) he gives us one of the Bible's most remarkable predictions.

He has already described the locusts and the drought that have afflicted his country as 'the day of the LORD'. This triggers for him the realization that that day is going to come again. For there is more to 'the day of the LORD' than his people have yet realized.

40

The Lord tells Joel, and Joel tells his readers, that another age is on its way. Having spoken to them about the events of their own age, he now describes what will happen 'afterwards' (verse 28) – 'in *those* days and at *that* time', 'in *that* day', as he will put it in the next chapter (3:1, 18). That will be the Lord's day, just as this time has been.

In one way the coming Lord's day will be like this one

Whatever Joel may have meant by signs in earth and sky and sun and moon, when he was commenting on the plague of locusts (verse 10), he says they will happen again on that future day (verses 30–31). (See *Black sun* (p. 42) for suggestions why the Bible uses this kind of language.)

In another way the coming Lord's day will be unlike this one

This little 'chapter 3' of Joel's book sandwiches his earth-and-sky, sun-and-moon prediction between two other predictions. He foretells an *outpouring* (verses 28–29) and a *rescuing* (verse 32). A more immediate outpouring and rescuing, which have to do with their present situation, are fresh in the minds of Joel's people; he has been speaking of them just a few verses back – verse 23 has described the rains which break the drought, and before that verse 20 has described Israel's deliverance from the locusts. But between the two outpourings there will be great differences, and between the two rescuings too. The 'day of the LORD' which is coming 'afterwards' will also bring an outpouring, but a far greater one – the outpouring of God's Spirit on all his people (verses 28–29). Furthermore, it will bring another rescuing – but again, one far greater: the salvation of all whom he calls, of all who call on him (verse 32).

What is so remarkable about this prophecy is that it puts in a nutshell what it means to be God's people in our own New

Testament times. Both Peter and Paul tell us that that is what Joel is predicting (Acts 2:16–21; Romans 10:12–13). Not only Jews, but everyone, can now call on the Lord and be saved. Not only prophets and priests and judges and kings, but everyone, can now receive his Spirit.

Questions

1. Why did Peter and Paul consider these verses so basic to the Christian good news? They came to see its deeper meaning; how much of that do you think Joel would have understood?
2. What signs of the Spirit's outpouring would you look for among God's people today?
3. How would you translate into evangelistic terms for the modern world Joel's promise that deliverance is to be found in Jerusalem? What does that mean for us?

Black sun, red moon, no stars?

The eye-popping descriptions in verses 30–31 look to us like an apocalyptic vision of the end of the world, such as we find in science fiction novels and films. The same sort of thing appears near the end of the Bible, in Revelation 6:12–13: 'There was a great earthquake. The sun turned black . . . the whole moon turned blood red, and the stars in the sky fell to earth . . .'. There it is called the great day of God's wrath, and it certainly does seem to be describing the end of the world. The words of Jesus in Matthew 24:29 are very similar, and have to do with 'the coming of the Son of Man'. Most Bible students believe that that 'coming' too means the return of Jesus at the end of history.

Some, however, would say that Jesus is there describing in vivid picture language not his own second coming, which as we now know was going to be at least 2000 years later, but something much more immediate, the events of AD 70. That was when a revolt by the Jews against the imperial power of Rome, which had long occupied the land of Israel, was brought to a bloody conclusion with first the siege and then the sack of their capital Jerusalem. In destroying the city, the Roman armies of Titus also effectively brought about the final downfall of the Jewish state. This catastrophe is what some believe is meant by the darkening of sun, moon, and stars which these prophecies speak of.

But what is the value of this picture language to us?

It labels a series of historic events in a particular way. For Joel, the day when the locusts came was like this; flying in their millions, the insects would literally have darkened the sun by day and the moon and stars by night, and earth and sky would have seemed to tremble at their coming. That identified it as 'the day of the LORD' (2:11). Long afterwards, on the Day of Pentecost, there was a great fulfilment of Joel's prophecy, not just because of the outpouring of the Spirit of God which everyone could see there and then (Acts 2:17), but because of the earthquake and the darkness which everyone would remember from seven weeks earlier, when the Son of God had died (Matthew 27:45–51). These things identified that first Passiontide/Easter/Pentecost as another, far greater, 'day of the LORD'.

So it could well be that when forty years later the old Jewish state finally collapsed, that also would be described metaphorically as an earth-shaking, light-quenching event, another hugely important 'day of the LORD' in the history of God's people. In any case, whether or not that is what Matthew 24:29 is about, the same sort of language certainly comes into its own when the book of Revelation uses it to describe the end of history. That will be the 'day of the LORD' in the fullest and final sense of the words.

Joel 3:1-8

All nations

The day of the LORD will be a day of judgment, and it will involve everyone, not just God's people.

Joel's first 'day of the LORD' was the time when God punished his people by inflicting locusts and a drought on them, made them admit their sin, and then put things right again for them.

These events provided a pattern for his description of another coming of 'the day of the LORD', some time in the future. Then all the 'locusts' and 'droughts' which are the result of sin, and which have afflicted God's people down the ages, would be finally dealt with.

In 3:1–8 God opens up one particular aspect of this: the removal of 'locusts'.

But he is not now speaking about irresponsible insects. There are human enemies of his people who are not irresponsible at all, but who know very well what they are doing. They are nations surrounding the kingdoms of Israel and Judah who repeatedly – not by instinct, like the locusts, but out of malice or greed – have caused trouble for God's people.

Among these 'locusts' God takes as his examples the three coastal powers whose territories lay between Israel and the

Mediterranean Sea – Tyre, Sidon, and Philistia (verse 4). These were among the most persistent trouble-makers during the time the Israelites existed as a nation in those parts.

It is true that God is 'writing the story', and causing events to happen so that they bring about his purposes. He makes use of Israel's pagan enemies, those human 'locusts', just as he uses the actual locusts, to discipline his own people – to punish them, to make them realize the folly of their ways, and to bring them to a better mind. But at the same time it is also true that the pagan nations involved don't believe in him, and don't recognize that he is using them for his own purposes. They really are free agents, doing what they want to do. And because they are not puppets, but really responsible for their wicked doings, they too are in line for God's judgment.

So when the final day of the LORD comes, and he gathers 'all nations' in 'the Valley of Jehoshaphat' (probably not a place called after the king of that name, but simply 'the place where *the LORD judges*' – which is what 'Jehoshaphat' means), Tyre and Sidon and Philistia will be there, and they will be punished.

The Bible repeatedly tells us that God is not just the Lord of his own people, but the God of all the earth. Most non-Christians today would say that even if he is real for those who believe in him, he isn't for those who don't. Most Tyrians and Philistines would have said the same about the God of Israel. But sooner or later, 'all nations' will find he is real, whether they have believed in him or not. That will be on the day when they are called to account before the judgment seat of this God.

Questions

1. Does verse 2 really mean that on the final 'day of the LORD' God will judge entire nations? And what exactly will he judge them *for*?
2. How does the tit-for-tat attitude of verses 4–8 square with

God's rule about loving enemies and turning the other cheek (Matthew 5:39–44)?

3. We rightly ask why it is that the arrogant, greedy, and violent so often seem to get away with their misdeeds. What is the answer of this passage (and of Psalm 73)?

Understanding Old Testament predictions

Two facts about Joel will help us to see how God wants to speak, not only to Joel's contemporaries, but also to us, through these prophecies.

Joel is limited in what he sees

Like all the prophets, when he predicts the future, he can see it only *from where he is in history*. He doesn't have the hindsight that we have, or the overview that God has. It is as though he is describing a range of distant mountains. Some peaks are obviously more distant than others, but he can't tell how much bigger or remoter one is than another.

With hindsight, we know that his prediction about the Spirit and salvation in 2:28–32 first came true on the day of Pentecost and has gone on being fulfilled ever since. But the general judgment of all nations (3:2) has still not happened, although twenty centuries have now gone by; while on the other hand, the judgment of Tyre, Sidon, and Philistia had already taken place more than three centuries before Christ. Joel nevertheless saw all these events as parts of the same 'mountain range'. They would all happen 'in those days and at that time' (verse 1).

In other words, Bible prophecy gives us a *view* of what God will do. We are not meant to use it as a *map* which will tell us in advance how he will fit it all together.

Joel is limited in what he knows

He takes it that God's people are the Israelites, God's land is Judah, God's city is Jerusalem, God's house is a building on Mount Zion. He may suspect that one day God will give all these terms a far deeper, broader meaning, but he doesn't know exactly how he will do it. In the same way God gives Ezekiel a prophecy about a rebuilt temple (chapters 40–47) and Amos one about a repaired 'tent of David' (9:11–12) because these are terms which they and their readers can relate to. Only in New Testament days will it become clear not just that all this is picture language for something much bigger (that, the prophets may well have realized), but that it represents the worldwide spread of the gospel of the kingdom of Christ.

So we always have to ask whether things foretold in the Old Testament come true literally (like the ones concerning the first coming of Christ), or in a much grander way than people might have thought at the time.

Joel 3:9–21

No unfinished business

The final coming of the day of the LORD will do away with evil, and bring back good, once and for all.

Once more the light of sun, moon, and stars fails, and earth and sky tremble. Here it is again, prophesied in the middle of Joel's final section (verses 15–16). It had happened in one way when the day of the LORD first brought the locusts (2:10). It was to happen in another way when the day of the LORD came another time, much later, to bring the outpouring of the Spirit and the offer of salvation for everyone – there it is in the middle of that section too (2:30–31). And it will happen this one last time when God brings history to an end.

What do we have in this passage on either side of the darkness-and-earthquake verses?

▶ Before them, the end of the 'locusts': the nations, the unbelieving world which has caused such trouble for God's people, finally dealt with (verses 9–14) – this is one aspect of 'the day of the LORD' (verse 14);

▶ After them, the end of the 'drought': all that God's people have had to do without, now made up to them (verses 17–21) – this is the other aspect of 'that day' (verse 18).

But the themes are intertwined. A 'harvest' figures also in the first part, in the judgment of the nations; but it is the grim harvest of God's enemies who are ripe for destruction (verse 13). His enemies figure also in the last part, in the picture of Judah's renewed fruitfulness; but simply to make a contrast, as their lands have become a desert (verse 19).

Both halves tell us that God leaves no unfinished business. He summons the wicked nations to do their worst, for 'in the valley of decision' his judgment is going to destroy them for good and all. He promises his people a security and a prosperity which are not only greater than any they have known, but which also will be theirs likewise for good and all.

We know that the completion of all these things is still in the future, even for us. The New Testament warns us against those who make out that the day of the LORD, in this ultimate sense, has already come (2 Thessalonians 2:2). In a way that Joel could scarcely have imagined, 'Egypt' and 'Edom' (verse 19) have become umbrella terms covering a worldwide, centuries-long opposition to God's kingdom, while 'Judah' and 'Jerusalem' (verse 20) now stand for the international church of Jesus Christ; but still evil seems overwhelming, and still good seems to be in short supply. But the final day of the LORD *will* come. And that encourages us in at least two ways:

- When we look around, and see far more evil and far less good in the world than there ought to be, Joel reminds us that this unsatisfactory state of affairs is not going on indefinitely. When the Lord comes in person to live among his people, the way things are at present will be finished with, and replaced by a whole new order (verses 15–16).

- When we look ahead, we glimpse the fact that that new order will be permanently right and good. There are too many Christians who *say* they look forward to the next world, but who privately think of it as less interesting and exciting – somehow *thinner* – than this world. The Bible assures us that the opposite is true!

Questions

1. If on the last day God is going to right all wrongs, what should we be doing about them in the meantime?
2. The individual believer can always 'say of the LORD, "He is my refuge and my fortress"' (Psalm 91:2). What extra meaning do the similar words in Joel 3:16 have? (See Hebrews 12:22–29.)
3. How do verses 18–21 help us to understand heaven?

OBADIAH THE TELLER OF HOME TRUTHS

Obadiah 1–21

Obadiah 1–9

The day of Edom

It may be gratifying to see the law catch up with your unpleasant neighbours, but you would be unwise merely to feel smug.

Obadiah's is the shortest book in the Old Testament, and he has the briefest introduction of all the prophets. We may not even know his name; 'Obadiah' means the servant  of Yah (the name of the God of Israel), so the heading in verse 1 could simply be 'The vision of the Lord's servant'. Nor do we know when he wrote. All we are told is that he was given a message 'about Edom'.

We have seen that Joel's prophecy was about his own people Israel. Now God tells us through Obadiah that he is as concerned with outsiders as with insiders. It is true the Edomites were only just outside, since they and the Israelites were closely related, being descended from the twin brothers Esau and Jacob respectively, sons of Isaac and grandsons of Abraham. Geographically too the Edomites were only just outside, being next-door neighbours to Israel. Their territory lay on the far side of the Jordan valley, in the region called Mount Seir. But if God is prepared to be tough with people so close to home, and tell them a few home truths, we know he will be as fierce if not fiercer with his more way-out opponents.

He speaks first about the day when Edom will be punished. Three things emerge concerning what he will do 'in that day' (verse 8), and the three are punctuated by the repeated words 'declares the LORD':

(verses 2–4) 'Pride goes before a fall'
  (declares the LORD),
(verses 5–7) 'There will be no picking up of the pieces'
  (declares the LORD),
(verses 8–9) 'Edom will collapse from within'.

To put these another way:

God sees a terrible sin in Edom (verses 2–4)

It was just an accident of history and geography, really. The ancestors of these Edomites had settled in a mountainous region. It was easily fortified, and it gave the nation a great sense of security. They were so proud of their mountain strongholds!

But God had said long before what he thought of that kind of arrogance, in the story of the Tower of Babel in Genesis 11:1–9. And as he would say long afterwards through his servant Paul, 'What do you have that you did not receive? . . . why do you boast . . . ?' (1 Corinthians 4:7).

You don't have to be an out-and-out pagan to get above yourself in this way. It is to Edom, not only a neighbour but a relative of Israel's, that God is speaking. Israel is intended to overhear, and to take warning about the dangers of having too high an opinion of yourself.

God threatens a terrible fate for Edom (verses 5–7)

Thieves take what they want and leave what they don't. Grape-pickers don't strip the vines completely. But Edom will be deprived of everything. Later, when God mentions the survivors of an Israelite disaster (verse 14), he will go on to say that by contrast, 'There will be no survivors from the house of Esau' (verse 18).

It is one of the great themes of the prophets that however Israel may suffer God will see to it that there is always a remnant left (we shall find this especially in the book of Micah). It will always be possible to pick up the pieces and start again. But no chance of that for Edom – there will be no pieces to pick up. Israel, overhearing Obadiah's prophecy, must realize how she herself could well deserve to forfeit everything, and how merciful God is if after all she doesn't.

God uses a terrible method against Edom (verses 8–9)

Edom's life will be sapped from the inside. God will take away its inner strength, the leadership of the wise and the valour of the warriors, and the basic advantage of its situation in the mountains. You might say that the nation will find itself without its backbone, or its lifeblood, and will collapse and die.

God's people, looking on, must learn from that too. How they should treasure the advantages God has given them! How easily they might become careless about the things that really matter, and wake up one day to find themselves in a similar state of collapse!

Questions

1. 'Pride' has several shades of meaning, ranging from self-respect to arrogance. What kinds are proper for the Christian, and what kinds are wrong?
2. What are the fundamental strengths without which a church will perish?

3. In the course of history God has caused many nations to disappear, leaving practically no trace behind. Who in today's world needs to be reminded of this fact? Which nations seem most likely to disappear and why?

Obadiah 10–14

The day of Israel

Edom has been not only arrogant but heartless. God hates heartlessness – especially towards those who should be near and dear to you.

In verses 1–9 Obadiah has spoken of the day when the nation of Edom is destroyed. We might call 'that day' (verse 8) the *day of Edom*, and might attach a corresponding label, the *day of Israel*, to the events described in the next five verses. Each of these two 'days' was a day of judgment, in the sense that something dreadful (but deserved) happened to Edom, and something very similar had already happened to Israel.

The 'day of Israel', however, was judgment day in a further sense. Before sentence is carried out on the criminal (which is one kind of judgment), it has to have been decided by the judge (which is another kind of judgment). What happened on the 'day of Israel' was two judgments, one of each kind – the law was executing the sentence against Israel, but also passing the sentence against Edom.

Judgment day can mean the day when your fate *arrives*

If verses 10–14 describe the 'day of Israel', it is because they are about God *carrying out* his judgment against Israel. Ten times Obadiah speaks of 'the day'. It is like the tolling of a bell. The NIV leaves out two of the bell-strokes, but the RSV has all of them:

▶ The day that you stood aloof . . . the day that strangers carried off his wealth . . . the day of your brother;

▶ The day of misfortune . . . the day of ruin . . . the day of distress;

▶ The day of calamity . . . the day of calamity . . . the day of calamity;

▶ The day of distress.

When was 'that day'? We don't know for certain. Nor do we need to know (see *The value of background information*, p. 57). But much the most likely guess is that it was the 'day', actually a period of about a month, when a series of Babylonian invasions of Judah reached their climax with the sacking of Jerusalem and the deporting of most of the inhabitants.

Judgment day can also mean the day when your fate *is decided*

In the very act of carrying out his judgment against Israel God is *deciding* his judgment on Edom. By the Edomites' attitude to 'the day of Israel' their own fate is settled.

And what is their attitude?

First gloating and glee at Israel's misfortune, then taking advantage of it and profiting from it, and in the end adding to it by their callous cruelty – all that is in verses 12–14.

But as the preceding verses have made plain, what is so bad about it is that it is violence *against a brother*. As Edom was called

'Esau' in verses 8–9, so Israel is called 'Jacob' in verse 10, because (as we have already noted) the two nations were descended from these two brothers. The really dreadful thing that Edom did on this occasion was to stand aloof as foreigners attacked Israel, and then to range himself not with his brother but with his brother's enemy. It was more than a betrayal; it was a decision to side not with 'the people' but with 'the nations' (to use the biblical terms which distinguish those who are and those who are not God's own people).

Questions

1. 'Love does not delight in evil' (1 Corinthians 13:6) as Edom gloated over Israel's misfortunes. How difficult do you personally find this ideal?
2. We are often challenged not to stand aloof while others suffer. Would you see any particular recent event as a parallel to that of these verses?
3. Would the New Testament agree that your destiny tomorrow may be settled for good and all by your decision today? Does God allow you to change your mind? Can you decide at a future date not to be saved?

The value of background information

When you first discover the fascination of Bible study, it makes you eager for extra information to fill out what the text in front of you says. Who was Obadiah? What was Edom? When did all these things happen?

Questions like this have different kinds of answers.

▶ The Bible itself may be able to tell you, as you read more of it and follow up cross-references and concordances and commentaries. For instance, other parts of the Bible outside Obadiah will explain where the nation of Edom came from.

▶ Those who study Bible background – that is, sources of information on Bible times from outside the Bible – may be able to tell you. For instance, historical and archaeological research will explain something (though not much) about how Edom eventually disappeared.

▶ Nobody may be able to tell you! For instance, nothing is known about Obadiah except what we learn from the book that bears his name.

▶ Nobody may be able to tell you, but the evidence may be enough for educated guesses to be made. For instance, when the Babylonians destroyed Jerusalem (as the Bible tells us) in 587 BC (as historical research tells us), that situation was one into which the events of Obadiah would fit very well.

Naturally we think, 'If only I had more background knowledge I should understand the Bible better'. Well, yes, in one way that would be true. But the way we are really meant to understand the Bible is different. Paul says that it is intended to instruct us for salvation, so that the man of God may be complete, equipped for every good work (2 Timothy 3:15–17, RSV). For *that* purpose we do have enough in the Bible as it stands. This is the great doctrine of 'the sufficiency of Scripture'. All we really need is here.

Obadiah 15–21

'The day of the LORD'

What happens to both Edom and Israel sets the pattern for the outcome of the whole of history.

 The last section of Obadiah begins with one of Joel's great themes (it will come to the fore again in Zephaniah). That is the day of the LORD.

Verses 8–10 spoke of the day of Edom's downfall. For Obadiah that day had not yet come. Verses 11–14 spoke of the day of Israel's downfall, which Obadiah had already seen. How does the day of verse 15 relate to these other two?

For Obadiah, both the day of Edom and the day of the LORD were still future, and looked as if they belonged together. And so they did in a sense. It is true that the Edomite nation disappeared long before the time of Christ, while the judgment of all nations has still not arrived twenty-five centuries later, so the day of Edom and the day of the LORD are a long way apart. But the one event is a preview and a pattern of the other. Obadiah naturally speaks in terms of his own place and time, but what he says about Edom and Israel ('Esau' and 'Jacob') helps us to see what the day of the LORD will mean on the one hand for those who reject God and on the other for those who love him.

The day of the Lord spells doom for Edom

Obadiah focuses on four aspects of the fate of Edom:

- Its punishment will fit its crimes, for God always acts with strict justice (verse 15);

- Its world will be turned upside down, so instead of a drink celebrating victory it has to drink a cup of suffering (verse 16);

- It will find that survival, holiness, and security belong after all to the despised people of God (verse 17);

- In contrast, it will find itself, once so superior, finally reduced to nothing. Edom betrayed the survivors of Israel's day of disaster (verse 14), but will itself have no survivors (verse 18).

The day of the Lord spells hope for Israel

On the positive side Obadiah has three kinds of expectation with regard to God's people:

- He foresees Israel spreading out from its very limited territory to become something like what it was in the golden age of King David (verse 19);

- He foresees Israelite exiles returning home, though the geography and history behind this are no longer quite clear (verse 20);

- He foresees authority at last in the hands of the Lord and his people (verse 21).

Just as the rest of the nations which Edom represents have not yet been judged in the way that verses 15–18 describe, so we have never yet seen the expansion, the restoration, and the authority of God's people in the way that verses 19–21 describe.

But we know (because the New Testament has told us so) that on the final day of the LORD we can expect the triumph of God's people to be universal, and 'the kingdom of the world' to 'become the kingdom of our Lord and of his Christ'. That is how Revelation 11:15 echoes Obadiah 21. That is the tremendous meaning behind Obadiah's local place-names in this last section.

The note on Joel 3:1–8 (*Understanding Old Testament predictions*, p. 46) applies to this passage too. It is as though the prophet looking into the future sees and describes a hilltop he recognizes, but in fact its outline is the shape of a great mountain, just as real though very much further off.

Questions

1. Does verse 15 mean that wickedness always brings its own punishment, or that the Lord brings it, or both?
2. If we believe that in our age 'God's people' are the church of Christ, what do we make of prophecies about its possessing territory?
3. Since this last part of Obadiah explicitly concerns 'all nations', how is its message to be got across to them?

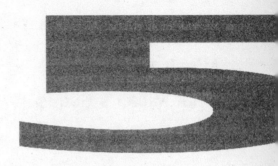

MICAH THE LEVELLER

Micah 1:1 – 2:13

Micah 1:1–2

What Micah's God is

Micah might well have quoted Psalm 95:3 to describe his God: 'The LORD is the great God, the great King above all gods.' In all the world there is none like him.

Micah's God is the same God as Joel's or Obadiah's, of course. He is the God of all the other prophets too. He is a God of law and grace, who lays down the law, which people proceed regularly to break, landing themselves in all sorts of trouble; and who then in grace – in undeserved kindness – leads them to repent and confess, and rescues them.

But each of the prophets was given his own personal vision of God. What is this God as Micah sees him? The answer is concentrated in the first two verses of his prophecy.

Micah's name tells us what this God is

'Micah' is a short form of 'Micaiah', which means 'Who is like the Lord?' There was a wide selection of gods to believe in during Old Testament times, but there was none quite like this one. First and most obviously, he was the only one who was actually alive! 'The Lord', or 'Yah' in Hebrew, was his name, and he was the God of the nation of Israel. 'Who-is-like-Yah?' was the name of his prophet.

Another Micah, a very different sort of man, had once installed in his home a god made of silver. The Bible writer points out how ironic this was – a heathen idol in the house of 'There's-no-one-like-Yah' (Judges 17:4 RSV)!

Micah's vision tells us what this God is

Micah is a man of the south – a man of Judah, that is, the more southerly of the two Israelite kingdoms – and his home is in the southern town of Moresheth. He prophesies in the reigns of three southern kings, and speaks of the southern capital Jerusalem. But for all that, he has a message for the north too, about the northern kingdom's capital Samaria. The word God gives him transcends historical and cultural boundaries, and people who don't recognize this God and who think quite differently from his prophet are nevertheless under his eye.

Micah's call tells us what this God is

Micah's vision concerns Samaria and Jerusalem, but he calls all peoples, everyone on earth, to hear what it is. So the God who gives it really is one who crosses boundaries, indeed frontiers. This is a universal summons to hear the word of the Lord. In all the world there is none like him.

There are as many lesser 'gods' in our day as there were in Micah's. Some are religious, but many are not. Ideas and principles and driving motives of all kinds, philosophical, political, psychological, govern the hearts and minds of our contemporaries. But Micah's incomparable God is infinitely greater than all of these, and will not be kept out of any area of human life.

Questions

---

1. Into what areas of your unconverted friends' lives do you think they would be most startled to have this God intrude? And which areas of your own?
2. God has accusations to make both against the unbelieving world and against the church. How might the realization of this affect the church's evangelism?
3. What would make you exclaim 'Who is like God?' Make individual lists and pool the answers or use a flip-chart and have a brainstorming session. What do you learn from your answers?

Micah 1:3–16

What Micah's God does

Don't imagine that this God shows either fear or favour. He deals even-handedly with everyone; he hates all sin, as much in his own city Jerusalem as in renegade Samaria.

Micah's incomparable God is a God who makes himself felt in our world. His coming down from heaven to earth is described vividly in verses 3–4, but what Micah is  describing in this way is in fact an invasion of Israelite territory by foreign armies. During the reigns of Jotham, Ahaz, and Hezekiah the great enemy dreaded by so many of the smaller nations of the Middle East was the Assyrian Empire. Several of its kings in turn brought their armies rampaging through what we think of as the Bible lands, and towards the end of the 8th century BC the northern kingdom of Israel was finally devastated and its capital Samaria destroyed. This, said Micah, was God's doing (verses 6–7).

But the Assyrian armies invaded Judah, the southern kingdom, also, and got as far as the gates of its capital (verses 9, 12). The places mentioned as being threatened by the enemy's line of march give Micah the opportunity for a series of grim puns (see p. 69).

How does Micah's special vision of God begin to emerge in these verses?

God has messages for everyone

Remember how Micah was introduced in verse 1. He is a man of the south, rooted in his own country and culture, but he is equally concerned for the north, and has a message for that community too, in spite of its alien life-style and ways of thinking.

He had the same outlook as Hezekiah, who was reigning in the south (alongside his father Ahaz) at the time when the northern kingdom collapsed, as verses 6–7 describe. Hezekiah hoped that the disaster would lead the survivors in the north to abandon the ancient quarrel, and rejoin the south (some did, some didn't). To him, and to Micah, the things the two communities had in common ought to have overridden the things that divided them.

This is God's outlook. The interests of every other god of the ancient world (like those of our world!) were more or less limited. This God is universal. He pronounces doom on those who refuse him (verses 6–7) as well as warning for those who may yet be saved (verses 8–16). He will level Samaria, in the sense that he will flatten the city and lay bare its foundations. In another sense he levels both kingdoms – he brings them to the same level, treating both equally as the objects of his concern;

the south is not above reproach, the north is not beneath contempt.

God has lessons for his own people

Where there are ears that will listen to him, he wants to encourage the hearers to have the same wide view – to have an eye to what is going on elsewhere – and to learn from it.

When Micah's people in the south see the ruin of the north, what might be their reaction? Horror and dismay? Indifference? Smug complacency? God says, 'Be warned. If I let such things happen *there*, there is no reason why they might not happen *here*,' and he brings the invader to the very gates of Jerusalem.

If on the other hand these people here are taken up only with their own welfare, with heeding God's warning and saving their own skins, and have turned their backs on those people there, he says, 'Don't be selfish. If I give *you* a chance to put things right, ought you not to be concerned that the same chance continues to be offered to *them*?'

Questions

1. In the light of this passage, on what areas of your life might God have some comment to make? How do you respond?
2. Can we tell whether any particular modern event might properly be described as 'the LORD coming down and making the mountains melt and the valleys split'?
3. The invasion which first ravages Samaria and then aims for Jerusalem is an example of any evil which may affect both secular society and the church. What would you say are present-day 'invasions' of this kind?

Micah's grim puns

Micah's first chapter is the tale of a disaster that spreads from the northern kingdom to the very heart of the southern one. It is not a tale to tell in the Philistine city of Gath, he says, echoing David's words 300 years before (2 Samuel 1:20). But it will be all too real to the towns of Judah, and he describes their reactions in words that sound like the towns' names. Starting with Beth Ophrah (and excluding Jerusalem, Peacetown, which was actually preserved during the invasion), these names sound something like Dust-town, Fairtown, Forthtown, Taketown, Bittertown, Teamtown, Bridetown, Cheat-town, and Oust-town. Adullam, at the end of the list, is (like Gath at the beginning) a harking back to the days of David and Saul – a mean hide-out mentioned in 1 Samuel 22:1 in which 'the glory of Israel' (its leading citizens) will have to take refuge.

Micah 2:1–13

What Micah's God sees

God's eyes range across the whole life of his people. He does hold out a hope for the future, but what about the sins of the here and now, all of them evident to him?

We know already that God is concerned with 'the sins of the house of Israel' in general (1:5). Now he becomes specific. 'Israel' to him means the nation as a whole, and he speaks to each of its two kingdoms equally. The fact that he is the incomparable God means among other things that he is not limited by frontiers, as other gods are. In the same way, within each kingdom he is concerned with every area of life, and will not be kept out of any. So throughout Israelite society he finds particular sins that have to be dealt with.

God sees specific sins

He pinpoints three evils in the Israelite communities, all of them not only offensive to him but harmful to Israel itself.

▶ Society is being damaged (verses 1–5). God has his eye on people who plan a particular kind of evil. It is the taking of the property of others by fraud, out of greed. It is done by people who are so powerful that they can get away with it in broad daylight (verse 1). But what is even more wrong about it is that in the process it breaks up the time-honoured system of inheritance (verse 2), a system which God had intended should keep Israel from ever suffering extremes of wealth and poverty.

▶ Truth is being distorted (verses 6–7). God hears those whose job it is to comment truthfully and fearlessly on current events soft-pedalling the less welcome truths they should be speaking. They are contradicting what Micah says, and denying that God would want him to say such things.

▶ People are being demoralized (verses 8–10). Here God is concerned, not so much for the poor, as he is in the prophecy of Amos, as for the middle class which is the backbone of the nation. What was the point of its thrift and honesty, now that it finds itself deprived of the decent clothes and homes it has worked for?

God responds to each situation

He will not leave any of these sins unpunished, and he responds to each as it deserves.

▶ Against those who plan evil, he says that he too will plan evil, using the same words in verse 3 as in verse 1.

▶ Against those who say he would never utter harsh and destructive words, he insists that his words do 'do good', but only 'to him whose ways are upright' (verse 7).

▶ From those who take away the blessings he has given to his people, he in turn will take away the blessing of a 'resting place' which he would otherwise have given them (verse 10).

God aims at a greater blessing

He goes back to the second of the three evils he has been exposing, the prophets who are supposed to speak truth to Israel and don't do it. What they say, because it is what Israel wants them to say, is basically about 'wine and beer', or the enjoyment of a satisfactory standard of living (verse 11).

What God says, however, and the message Israel really *needs* to hear, is much more radical and far-reaching. It has to do with the preserving of a remnant and the shepherding of a flock. Micah combines these two great Bible themes as a marker with which he will round off each of the four sections of his book. At the end of this first one the gathering of the remnant of his people into a sheepfold is not, taken by itself, quite the picture they will find helpful, since they are already in the claustrophobic situation of being threatened with a siege, as the enemy approaches Jerusalem; so here the King, the LORD, is promised as one who having gathered them will then lead them *out* to safety. But either way the message is one of infinitely greater worth than a mere promise of wine and beer! It is a challenge to stand against the trend of society, and to be one of the minority, the remnant which allows itself to be directed by God as its Shepherd-King.

Questions

1. The sins in this chapter are primarily those of people in positions of power and authority. How can the church address them both prophetically and practically?
2. We may not see ourselves as being guilty of such sins, but in what ways might we recognize the seeds of them in our own hearts?
3. Granted that verse 11 is a caricature, what kind of preaching in the church is being satirized by it?

MICAH THE LIFTER

Micah 3:1 - 4:8

Micah 3:1–12

Judgment on the mountain

Micah lifts our eyes to the church, which is meant to be 'a city on a hill', an outstanding testimony to God's greatness. Is it after all just 'a heap of rubble'?

Micah's God is an incomparable God, so we must on no account limit him to the first impressions we may have formed of him. We now come to the second section of the prophecy, and new aspects of him come to light.

God's message is for the secular world, true, but also for the church

What he and his prophet Micah had seen in Judah and Jerusalem was a range of social evils, involving particularly the leadership of Israelite society. God's judgment on such things needs to be applied to any society in any age, whether or not it claims to be based on biblical principles. We ourselves ought to probe our own national life in the light of it.

But we must never forget that the kingdom of Judah was something more than a nation state. In that day and age it was the form taken by God's own people, and from this point of view not one of the nation states of today is its equivalent, not even the modern state of Israel, but the church of Jesus Christ. So it is church structures and leadership even more than social or national life that God expects us to probe in the light of chapter 2.

God's messenger is a 'leveller', true, but also a 'lifter'

Unlike any other god, this God is concerned with all nations equally, as we have seen. He deals with them all on the same level – none is either above or beneath his notice (1:1–2).

But Micah says plainly that in another sense one of them *has* been raised above all the others. Israel has been given very special privileges, and very special responsibilities. Not for nothing was it a hilltop town, Jerusalem, which God chose to be his people's capital and the site of his own house, the temple. Several of the Psalms (48, 68, 87, 125, among others), also lift our eyes to God's 'holy mountain'. Long afterwards Jesus will tell his people, 'You are the light of the world. A city on a hill cannot be hidden . . . Let your light shine before men, that they may see your good deeds and praise your Father in heaven' (Matthew 5:14, 16).

So Jerusalem, representing the church, is the object of a message both of judgment (3:1–12) and of hope (4:1–8). Some English translations hide the connection between 3:12 and 4:1 – 'the temple hill', says one verse; 'the mountain of the LORD's house', says the next, according to the New English Bible – but Micah deliberately used the same words in both verses, so that the judgment chapter ends and the hope chapter begins with the same focus, the 'mountain of the house' (that is the LORD's house, the Jerusalem temple).

There is a message of judgment on the mountain

God, through Micah, is saying the same kind of thing that he said in chapter 2.

▶ Verses 1–4 are addressed to leaders and rulers again, those who have power over others and enrich themselves at the expense of others, as in 2:1–5.

▶ Verses 5–8 are addressed to 'prophets', to communicators and commentators, those 'who speak what many hear and write what many read', as in 2:6–7.

▶ Verses 9–12 are addressed to the destructive system in general, as in 2:8–10. Now priests are included as well as leaders and prophets, all united in injustice, cruelty, greed, and spiritual blindness.

However, although the message here is broadly the same as that of the previous chapter, in this one it comes clearly into focus as a message for *God's people*. It is social ills in the body of the nation which are being judged; but this happens to be God's own holy nation, and the 'mountain of the house' is supposed to be uplifting a revelation of God's truth which all other nations can look up to!

Instead, says Micah to these (as we should call them) Christian leaders, 'Because of you . . . Jerusalem will become a heap of rubble', the mountain of the house a wilderness, and the witness of the church totally compromised in the eyes of the watching world.

Questions

1. Among the sins exposed here, greed and avarice are the most prominent (verses 2–3, 5, 11). In what ways do you think you might be in danger of falling into these sins? How can you escape them?
2. We are shown God's reaction to his people's sin in verses 4, 8, and 12. How might this be experienced in one of today's churches?
3. To what extent can you truthfully say, 'I am no leader, these judgments are not aimed at me'?

Micah 4:1–8

Hope on the mountain

The Lord holds out hope for all the nations. But they will find it only on his mountain, among his people.

 In Micah's time the city on the hill was a poor advertisement for the glory of God. In the end it became literally what all too often it was metaphorically – in a moral and spiritual sense, 'a heap of rubble', not worth lifting your eyes to look at. So said the last verse of chapter 3. Yet it will still be there 'in the last days', says the first verse of this next chapter. It will be possible to lift your eyes to the 'mountain of the LORD's house' and to see there not judgment but hope – what is more, hope not only for God's people, but also for you, if you are not yet one of them.

The future holds a hope

It is a hope for all the nations. It belongs to the last days, which means the period following the coming of Christ (so Peter on the day of Pentecost explains the parallel prophecy in Joel; Acts 2:16–21; Joel 2:28–32). All through that time the life-giving 'word of the LORD' will be spreading across the world 'from Jerusalem', its source (verse 2). At the end of that time will arrive the fulfilment of the famous prophecy of verse 3b: 'They will beat their swords into ploughshares and their spears into pruning hooks. Nation will not take up sword against nation, nor will they train for war any more.'

The hope includes more than that, because Micah outlines not one but four freedoms. They are not quite the four that Franklin D. Roosevelt looked forward to after World War 2, but they are similar:

- freedom from injustice (verse 3a)

- freedom from war (verse 3b)

- freedom from want (verse 4a)

- freedom from fear (verse 4b).

This text (verses 3–4, but especially verse 3b) is often lifted out of its context. As always when a part of Scripture is treated in this way, we have to look at the passage as a whole to see how the 'No more war' promise will come true. The answer is not what politicians commonly think.

The hope of the nations depends on Israel

This refers to Israel, of course, in the biblical sense – that is, the people of God, all who are his by faith. Ever since Jerusalem became God's city, indeed ever since Israel became God's nation, they were meant to be 'the pillar and foundation of the truth', as Paul calls the church in 1 Timothy 3:15. In Micah 3 they were failing to be what they should be. But God knew that a day would come when they would once again 'hold out the word of life' (Paul again – Philippians 2:16), and there would be people of all nations who would realize that their only hope lay in going 'up to the mountain of the LORD' and learning among his people 'his ways' and 'his paths'.

The promise of the four freedoms is inextricably woven in

with the fabric of God's teaching and law and judgment and word and name. Only as they throw in their lot with God's people is there any true hope for the nations of the world.

And why should God's people, failures that they are, themselves have any hope?

The hope of Israel depends on the Lord

It is he who will put all things to rights 'in that day', gathering, assembling, strengthening, ruling, and restoring (verses 6–8). Israel's part, and ours, is to accept that he alone can do all these things, and to trust wholeheartedly in him to do them for us.

The two pictures of the remnant and the flock reappear at the climax of this section as they did at the end of the first one (2:12–13). There are new depths to both of them: *strength* in the case of the remnant (to be made a remnant means in this case not 'to be all but destroyed', but 'to be certain of survival'), *security* in the case of the flock (it has as a magnificent watchtower the strong city of Jerusalem itself).

Well, the last days are now here, though not yet the last day of all, and the challenge is still to God's people to be the kind of city on a hill which draws others to the Lord rather than turning them from him.

Questions

1. What signs do we see of many nations wanting to learn God's ways? Or are verses 1–2 still unfulfilled?
2. How realistic would it be for verse 3 to be part of a political manifesto?
3. 'Lame' in verse 7 is a very rare word; almost the only other place it occurs is in Genesis 32:31. Reading this Micah verse in connection with that Genesis story, how might a personal sense of being 'lame' or 'a remnant' be of positive spiritual value?

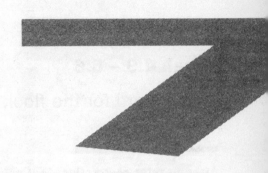

MICAH THE
CAROL SINGER

Micah 4:9 – 5:15

Micah 4:9 – 5:6

A Shepherd for the flock

After disaster, restoration – but only when the promised Shepherd-King arrives.

At last we arrive at a prophecy which every Bible reader will recognize. It is almost as if Micah bursts into song: 'O little town of Bethlehem', he carols, in a passage which Christians instantly connect with the birth of Jesus 700 years after Micah's time.

This famous verse (5:2) is at the centre of the third section of his book, in which he is showing how God takes his people through trouble and out the other side – through fire and water and out to a place of abundance, as Psalm 66:12 puts it. The theme of the shepherded flock comes to the fore in this first half of the section, and that of the preserved remnant will do so in the second half.

Three messages for Jerusalem

Not all the translations make it clear, but 4:9–10 is one message, 4:11–13 a second, and 5:1–6 a third. Each begins with the word 'Now'; each speaks to the city of Jerusalem (the 'Daughter of Zion'), representing God's people; and each promises a triumphant outcome out of deep trouble. The gist of all three is: 'Now, in spite of your distress, Jerusalem, I am going to do something very special for you.'

The three prophecies run something like this:

► 'Now you cry, believing (wrongly) that you have been abandoned. But what you are suffering is the pains of childbirth, which have a happy end result. You are going eventually to be exiled to Babylon, but only to experience God's rescue from there' (4:9–10).

► 'Now many wicked nations (represented by the Assyrian invader) are gathered against you. But God has brought them here simply for you to destroy them!' (4:11–13).

► 'Now you have been attacked and besieged. But I will save you through my chosen ruler, who will come from Bethlehem, whose birth is what these labour-pains are heralding, who will be the great Shepherd-King, and whose followers will dominate the nations' (5:1–6).

The message for Bethlehem (5:2)

This is included within the third message to Jerusalem, like one letter enclosed in another.

What would Micah's contemporaries have made of his words to Bethlehem?

Obviously it wouldn't have been the Christmas scene which instantly opened up before their eyes! On the other hand, *something* did. 'You, Bethlehem,' said Micah, 'out of you will come for me one who will be ruler over Israel', and they would not have been at a loss as to what he *might* mean. (There are few if any Old Testament prophecies which would have meant nothing at all to those who heard them at the time.)

They would probably have understood this one as follows. In the days of the kings of Judah Bethlehem was thought of, as another of our Christmas carols puts it, as 'royal David's city'. So when Micah spoke of the coming time when God would put things right for his people, and said that he would do it through a ruler who would originate from Bethlehem, he could have meant a king of Jotham's and Ahaz's and Hezekiah's line (1:1), since their ancestor David was born in Bethlehem, even if they themselves weren't. Or again, if a few years after this prophecy Hezekiah had had a grandson (say) who for some reason was actually born in Bethlehem instead of Jerusalem, and another messenger like Micah had said that that child was to be the promised Rescuer, God's chosen one, his hearers would not have been surprised. If he had quoted a verse from yet another of our carols, it would have made sense to them:

> To you in David's town this day
>   Is born of David's line
> A Saviour, who is Christ

– though the next two words, saying that the baby prince was himself 'the Lord', *would* have shocked and mystified them.

When eventually Jesus was born, and wise men from the east came asking where the new king would be, the pundits in Jerusalem had no hesitation in quoting Micah 5:2. Not that they were going to recognize Jesus as the coming Rescuer! 'He came to that which was his own, but his own did not receive him' (John 1:11). It tells us a lot about prophecy, and about God's word in general, that a prediction could be so precise and yet that men who knew all about it could fail to see what it implied when it actually came true.

Micah's incomparable God was pointing to a fact which no other god can claim – that he who made the world was going to be born into it, like the men he had created, and he even specified the village where this miracle of miracles would happen.

1. In what sense does the promise to Jerusalem in 4:13 ('You will break to pieces many nations') come true?
2. 'She who is in labour' (5:3) seems to mean the Old Testament church, the 'mother' from whom Jesus was born. If 5:4–6 are about the New Testament church, what might be symbolized by its raising up 'shepherds' and 'leaders' against 'Assyrian invaders'?
3. The more vividly we picture the birth of Jesus, the harder it is to imagine him creating the universe long before, and vice versa. At Christmas, how readily can you bring together in your mind the baby of Bethlehem and the one 'whose origins are . . . from days of eternity' (5:2, NIV margin)?

Prediction and fulfilment

It is easy to misunderstand how the predictions of God's prophets work, and how they are meant to be used. I believe many Christians take it for granted that predictive prophecy operates something like this:

▶ **At the time of the prediction**, a prophet would describe a future event, and his prophecy would be noted and put by. In due course something would begin to happen which seemed to resemble what he had predicted, the prophecy would be taken off the shelf, dusted down, and compared with current events, and if they were found to tally, everyone would recognize that the prophecy was being fulfilled.

That was not in fact what usually happened, and Micah 5:2 is a case in point!

➤ **At the time of the fulfilment**, it is assumed that an equally simple process takes place. Again taking the Bethlehem prophecy as an example, when God (to put it crudely) was arranging for his Son to be born, he had to decide among other things where it should happen. Then he remembered Micah 5:2, so he caused the birth to take place at Bethlehem, in order to fulfil the prophecy.

While this may be a caricature of the assumptions I am talking about, it does serve to show by contrast the real place of prediction in God's scheme of things. His whole plan is integrated and all of a piece – less like a random puzzle with arbitrary clues, more like a superbly plotted detective story in which the clues are available for all who will take the trouble to find them, and grow organically out of the situation and the characters. Readers in tune with the author's mind will realize on reflection why he plants Micah 5:2 (for example) where he does, and why it is an inevitable link (not an arbitrary one) between Old Testament and New.

The popular but misguided view of prophecy would say that any town would have been as good as any other for God to decide on as the birthplace of his chosen King, so long as he made Micah's prophecy and Matthew's gospel agree. The true view requires us to unravel the plot with care and logic, asking ourselves from what nation, from which tribe in that nation, from whose family in that tribe, and therefore from which town, the chosen King was likely to come.

We should not see God as the manipulator of events to make them fit in with Scripture. Rather we see Scripture as revealing to us all that we need to know about God's wonderful plans.

Micah 5:7–15

A Preserver for the remnant

God preserves his people, in order to use them as his messengers in the world.

How will the remnant be preserved? The short answer is, God will preserve it.

But we can really do with a fuller answer than that. The word 'remnant' has such a forlorn sound about it; and from one point of view the remnant of Israel is rightly described as the shreds, the pitiable leftovers, of a once great nation. That sort of remnant, a wretched, dispirited bunch of refugees, the Lord does indeed preserve, by providing care and shelter for them. But the preserving of the sort of remnant that Micah has in mind is an altogether more bracing affair. This remnant, of course, is the true people of God, in New Testament terms the true church. God preserves it not only by doing something *for* it but by doing something *to* it. These people will survive not in spite of their feebleness, but because of their *toughness*, and they are tough because God has made them so. Verses 7–9 tell us about his purpose, and verses 10–15 about his method.

He intends to use them (verses 7–9)

He makes them strong to survive because he has purposes in the world for which they are to be his instruments. The purposes are of two kinds:

▶ Constructively, he will make them 'like dew' and 'like showers', which come to water the crops, and which come by God's grace, not at man's bidding.

▶ Destructively, he will make them 'like a lion', which comes to maul and mangle, as much beyond human control as the dew and the rain are.

The New Testament too uses picture language to describe all this. Revelation 11 speaks of the two irrepressible witnesses who testify unceasingly to God's truth in this wicked world, and who even when their enemies kill them come back to life. 2 Corinthians 2:14–16 uses the unlikely metaphor of the 'smell' of Christ! The church's witness is a life-giving fragrance to those who are prepared to respond to it, and a death-dealing stench to those who refuse it.

The indestructible witnesses correspond to the remnant, God's tough survivors, and the two kinds of smell correspond to the life-giving dew and the death-dealing lion. This double ministry is the purpose for which God preserves his true people.

Something further is in his mind if they are going to be effective in carrying out this purpose. That is the method by which he prepares them.

He intends to discipline them (verses 10–15)

There is such a harsh change of tone at verse 10 that we might wonder whether the Lord is still speaking to Israel and Jerusalem, especially to the remnant which is so close to his heart and so important to his plans. But yes, he is continuing to address his own people, and it is precisely because of his plans for them that he now speaks so harshly. Because he wants to use them, he must discipline them.

Here then is more destruction, not among Israel's enemies (to that, the end of each section refers – verses 9 and 15), but within Israel itself. But note what it is he intends to destroy (demolish, tear down, uproot, there is no mistaking his intention!). Lined up for radical surgery are:

▶ horses, chariots, cities, strongholds – all reliance on military strength (verses 10–11);

▶ witchcraft and spells – all reliance on the occult (verse 12);

▶ carved images, sacred stones, Asherah poles, altars (NEB) – all reliance on false religion and idolatry (verses 13–14).

In other words he is determined to cut out of his people's life every confidence except confidence in him. Only those who are wholeheartedly committed to him are usable by him in the wicked world of which verses 9 and 15 speak.

Questions

1. In what sense may the three false confidences of verses 10–14 need to be dealt with in your own life?
2. How can the church be effective in its dual responsibility to the world, of being both 'like the dew' and 'like the lion'?
3. Can disasters be called 'discipline' if ungodly people refuse to see God's hand in them? Indeed, are Christian people more likely to see discipline of this kind than non-Christians? What events are discipline and what just accidents?

MICAH THE BRINGER OF JUDGMENT AND HOPE

Micah 6:1 – 7:20

Micah 6:1–7

A shaft deflected

**When the Lord aims accusations against us,
we naturally do our best to turn them aside.**

This is the beginning of the fourth and last
section of Micah's book (6:1 – 7:20). It has a
number of features we shall not be surprised
to find here.

- ▶ Micah has already used as a double marker the picture language of the shepherded flock and the preserved remnant, as he has moved to the climax of each of the earlier sections. They are here too (7:14, 18).

- ▶ In each section there has been a message of judgment followed by a message of hope. In fact they are the two great themes of his book as a whole, as of many of the prophetic books. They are here too: judgment in 6:1 – 7:6, hope in 7:7–20.

- ▶ Behind all his prophecy we have been aware of his own special vision of the Lord as the incomparable God. As it was spelt out at the beginning in the form of Micah's own name (1:1), it will be spelt out even more clearly at the end, in 7:18: 'Who is a God like you?'

▶ Again, as the book began with a courtroom scene, so it ends with one. In 1:2 God brings a charge against the world in general. What he has against it is now seen in close-up, as he brings a charge against Israel in particular. God instructs Micah, as prosecuting counsel on his behalf (6:1), and Micah accordingly addresses the everlasting hills, which were there before Israel ever came on the scene, as the jury (6:2).

The Lord accuses Israel (verses 3–5)

We are not given the specific accusation yet. That will come later (indeed we have a fair idea already from chapters 2 and 3 of what the charge sheet will look like). For the moment the Lord lists, not what they have done to him, but some of the things he has done for them – as if to say, 'How *could* you behave in the way you have, when I have been so gracious to you?'

▶ When they were enslaved in Egypt, he rescued them.

▶ When they were leaderless, he gave them Moses and his brother and sister to lead them.

▶ When the king of Moab tried to curse them, he turned the curse into a blessing.

▶ When they faced the perils of their new land, he brought them safely across Jordan, 'from Shittim to Gilgal', into it.

This was not a random assortment of kindnesses. These events sum up the 'saving acts of the LORD' (verse 5, RSV) at the time of the exodus, the prime example and the model of all he will ever do for his people.

In spite of this they were living lives that showed they cared nothing for him. Behind their many specific sins, this was the basic evil of which he was accusing them.

Israel deflects the accusation (verses 6–7)

God's people, like so many today who would call themselves Christians, reckon that they know how to answer these accusations and to show that they really do care about God. The answer is *religion*. More religion. More and better gifts for God, thousands of animals, even humans, for ritual slaughter, oceans of oil for offerings. As we might say, we must improve our Sunday services and multiply our church activities. If God is angry with us, this must be the way to win back his approval.

People who think like that have not understood a word God has been saying. They still believe, deep down, that they must *buy* his favour. When he reminds them of what he has done for them in the past – in Old Testament times, the exodus; in New Testament times, the cross – they simply assume that he means they must pay retrospectively, as it were. His rescues are a 'have now, pay later' arrangement. They seem incapable of grasping that the rescues were *free*, and that what God wants is not payment but a response of grateful obedience, which is not religious observance but quality living.

Since Israel wilfully misunderstands his first accusation, he will next set out their sin and their punishment in a way they cannot miss.

Questions

---

1. Do God's people ever have reason to complain that the Lord has 'burdened' them (verse 3)? Give examples.
2. Old Testament Israel was repeatedly urged to remember the events of the exodus. In what ways is the death of Jesus the New Testament counterpart of that, and how in practice should Christians 'remember' this?
3. Why is the attitude of verses 6–7 so common among religious people? How can it be avoided?

Micah 6:8 – 7:6

A shaft that strikes home

When the Lord's accusations become more explicit, honesty may make us admit that they are true.

 The way the NIV and other translations divide up and give headings to their paragraphs is not necessarily the way God intends these books to be read. Sometimes the meaning becomes clearer when we ignore these 'helps'. For instance, Micah 6:8 is usually assumed to belong with verses 6–7, but it is easier to see who is saying what to whom if we take it to belong with verses 9–16. (In the same way we shall detach 7:7 from what precedes it and read it as the introduction to what follows it.)

These paragraphs, then, are the Lord's second accusation, spoken through the mouth of his representative Micah, and followed by a response very different from that of 6:6–7.

The Lord accuses Israel again (6:8–16)

Step by step his charge against his people is opened out, until not only the crime but its consequences are plain.

▶ There can be no excuse for not knowing in the broadest

sense what God wants, and has not been getting: namely, 'what is good' – what I called in the last section quality living (6:8a). There is plenty in the Old Testament law about religious observances, certainly, but they are clearly only the 'outward and visible signs' of an 'inward and spiritual grace', which is the godly character God expects in his people.

▶ Practical goodness means, in the famous words of 6:8b, 'to act justly and to love mercy and to walk humbly with your God'. All three aspects of goodness were in short supply in Micah's Israel. Instead there was corruption and ruthlessness and an arrogant walking in one's own way.

▶ In even more practical terms God condemns the way these opposites of goodness work out in commerce and finance (6:9–12).

▶ In consequence God will hit them where it hurts, and all their gains will become losses (6:13–15).

▶ When the punchline compares the people of Judah to Omri and Ahab, those wicked kings of the north, it is condemning their greed and selfishness (see 1 Kings 21), pillorying them as a people just as wicked as their northern neighbours, and threatening them with the same fate as the northern kingdom, a fate which is all too fresh in their minds.

This time the accusation strikes home (7:1–6)

It is not that the Israelites of the southern kingdom have suddenly seen the error of their ways. It is simply that Micah, having so far spoken for God in the courtroom drama, now speaks for the nation, standing in the dock with them. It is all true. There is no godliness, no goodness, left, either on the national scene (7:1–4) or on the domestic front (7:5–6).

Micah knew of course that the ills of his society, which as an

Israelite himself he had to confess, were only the symptoms of a deep-seated disease. There is a danger in looking at 6:8 too superficially. Justice and mercy (if not humility) have today become fashionable. Among good-hearted people this verse can subtly become a basis for self-congratulation – 'We at any rate are doing our best to meet God's requirements.' But self-congratulation is not what it was for. It was meant as a *condemnation*. See the hidden depths of the three words:

▶ Justice actually means a life of *total righteousness*;

▶ Mercy is 'steadfast love', or a *total constancy* of caring;

▶ Humility is a *total submission*, moment by moment, to the wisdom of God.

These are huge demands! We are expected to meet them practically, in daily life, with God's help, as best we can. We are expected to champion, as many do, causes of justice and mercy in our society. But we are also expected to grasp that this threefold 'goodness' is not only a social thing, but a spiritual and personal one, and should affect *every* part of us. When we realize how repeatedly we fail in it, we are on the way to recognizing what sinners we are in God's sight, and that in turn underlines for us what a Saviour he is.

Questions

1. Faced with the three challenges of justice, mercy, and the humble walk with God, which do you find the hardest? Why?
2. Where in our society are the short measures and the false weights of 6:10–11 to be found? Are they in evidence even in 'God's city', the church? What is to be done about them?
3. The evils in Israel, and their consequences, touch Micah's heart (7:1). How much of an emotional reaction to such things can God expect in his people? Do you share it?

Micah 7:7–20

Confidence in the incomparable God

When we see the truth about how God's anger and mercy work, everything – present troubles and future hope – falls into place.

Verse 7 leads out of darkness into light. Micah would not unsay any part of the confession of sin in verses 1–6, but he now looks at the facts in the light of faith. The rest of his prophecy is in the form of a psalm (see *Psalms by unofficial psalmists*, p. 100).

This day's confidence (verses 8–10)

In this first section of the psalm the prophet speaks again, as he did in verses 1–6, on behalf of his people, perhaps specifically the people of the city of Jerusalem ('she who' is her enemy in verse 10 would, in that case, be either the capital city of Assyria (see p. 106), her attacker in Micah's time, or Babylon, her eventual destroyer (see p. 122)). When they see things clearly, they can accept the distress of the present day – it will be even worse a century later, when the city and nation really do fall – as God's anger because of his people's sin. They can also see that though God brought about these invasions, he is equally angry with the invaders, and will in due course punish them too.

That day's promise (verses 11–13)

Having spoken *for* his city and nation, the prophet now speaks *to* them. The 'day of the LORD', which looms large in the writings of other prophets, peeps through here also. It will be the day when God's people have finally been put right with him, and find the walls of their 'sheepfold' extended to welcome incomers from every other nation. Those who are still determined to stay outside will perish.

The flock shepherded (verses 14–17)

Now Micah speaks to the Lord, and the Lord answers him. The exodus is again the pattern for what God will do in that day, as he says in verse 15. He was the Shepherd of his people then (see Psalm 78:52–53) and later (Psalm 78:68–72). So he is in our time (John 10:11–16), and will be through all eternity (Revelation 7:13–17).

The remnant forgiven (verses 18–20)

'I believe in the forgiveness of sins, the resurrection of the body, and the life everlasting,' says the creed, and that is how God preserves the remnant. We have already seen that they survive because he gives them the strength and toughness to survive. But he does this by taking away the debilitating disease of sin and giving them an indestructible new life. How this is achieved is the heart of gospel truth, and brings us back to the cross of Christ. There is no other faith which can meet this ultimate need, no other God who can thus 'hurl all our iniquities into the depths of the sea' – only the incomparable God whose ways Micah has been setting before us.

Do you know the 18th century hymn based on verse 18? In it Samuel Davies uplifts above every other aspect of God's greatness the grace by which he rescues dying sinners and makes them into ever-living saints:

Great God of wonders, all thy ways
Are matchless, godlike and divine;
But the fair glories of thy grace
More godlike and unrivalled shine:
Who is a pardoning God like thee?
Or who has grace so rich and free?

Questions

1. Make a list of the circumstances in which you have been able (or now wish you had been able!) to feel the confidence of verse 8.
2. In the day of the LORD, the wonders with which he will bless the church and shame the world are described in terms of the flock (verse 14) and the exodus (verse 15). What things of this kind is it right to ask of him here and now?
3. How should verses 18–20 affect our methods of evangelism?

Psalms by unofficial psalmists

The book of Psalms is by no means the only place where we find these biblical songs or poems. Other psalms of David are to be found elsewhere (2 Samuel 1, 22, 23), and the Old Testament contains songs of Moses (Exodus 15; Deuteronomy 32) and Hezekiah (Isaiah 38), and prayers in the form of psalms by the prophets Jonah (Jonah 2), Nahum (Nahum 1:2–8), and Habakkuk (Habakkuk 3). Hannah's song (1 Samuel 2) was the model for Mary's in the New Testament, and that and the other two 'psalms' in Luke 1 and 2 came into regular use in Christian worship alongside the Old Testament collections.

Every Israelite child would have been steeped in the language and rhythms of such poetry, which is why (even in human terms, and still more when they were moved by the Spirit of God) there is nothing odd about the peasant girl Mary or the half-drowned prophet Jonah producing the memorable verses they did.

NAHUM THE
DENOUNCER

Nahum 1:1 – 3:19

Nahum 1:1

'Naught for your comfort'?

Nahum is a very uncomfortable book – or is it?

'Naught for your comfort' – the words are old-fashioned, but they stick in the mind. G. K. Chesterton coined the phrase, and Trevor Huddleston borrowed it for the title of  his famous book about apartheid in South Africa. At first sight the words might equally well suit the prophecy of Nahum, who describes just as grim a situation as these more recent writers.

The opening verse of his prophecy will help us to see the rest of it in the right light. So in a sense this section is about a single verse, but in another sense it is about the whole book. Read it straight through now; the three chapters will take only a few minutes.

* * * * *

It *is* grim, you see. It is full of fierceness and anger, gore and slaughter, suffering and desolation. Worse, the spirit in which all this is described is not a spirit of horror and dismay. It is one of gloating and hatred.

It has to be said that Nahum is a deeply unpleasant book. People who claim the Old Testament is full of violence and hatred often have no idea of what it actually says, but you need look no further than Nahum to find the sort of thing they have in mind.

The first verse of chapter 1 gives us the clues as to why such a book is in our Bibles. We know nothing about Nahum except what we may pick up from his book and nothing about Elkosh except that it was presumably in the territory of Judah, whose sister-kingdom Israel had already been destroyed when the book was written. But he had a vision from God, and wrote it down, and it was called 'an *oracle*', or a *burden*, 'concerning Nineveh'. It was *for* God's people the Israelites, but it was *about* their enemies the Assyrians (see *Nineveh and Assyria* below).

Nahum is writing about the Assyrians

An 'oracle' means of course a message from God. The word 'vision' or 'revelation' in the second half of the verse says the same thing. But the older translations were not wrong in calling it a 'burden'. It is both weighty and unpleasant. It will be a burden, however, not for Israelites but for Assyrians. It is they who will feel the weight of God's hand when he finally punishes them for their cruelty.

So 'naught for your comfort'?

Nahum is writing for the Israelites

For them the message really is a 'comfort'. There is nothing comfortable about it, certainly, but in the old sense of the word, it will strengthen and encourage them. God *will* one day put an end to suffering and punish the people who cause it.

Questions

1. How far can a Christian take comfort in the destruction of evil, even when it involves evil people? How far can we delight in a 'just war'?

2. In what circumstances would a modern preacher be justified in preaching from this book?
3. Who in more recent history might Nahum have bracketed with the Assyrians? (This is not as simple as it sounds.)

Nineveh and Assyria

(See the map on p. 18.)

Assyria, the super-power of the Middle East in the 7th century BC, is not named until almost the end of the book (3:18). The name of the city which was its seat of government, Nineveh, stands for the nation, just as we speak of 'Washington' and 'Moscow' to mean the USA and Russia.

Of all the Israelites' enemies, from the time of the exodus when they escaped from Egypt to the time of the exile when they were taken captive to Babylon, this one was the most feared and hated. Assyria was a byword among all the nations of the ancient Middle East for its inhuman atrocities. As the last verse of the prophecy will put it, 'Who has not felt your endless cruelty?'

It is easy to confuse Assyria with Syria, which was also at various times an enemy of Israel's. But the two are quite distinct. Syria was much the smaller of the two, a nation similar in size to Israel and adjoining it on its northern frontier. Assyria by contrast was a vast empire.

It collapsed in the end before the growing power of Babylon, which took its place as the dominant power in the Middle East (see *Babylon*, p. 122). The fall of the Assyrian capital, Nineveh, in 612 BC marks the end of one empire and the triumph of the next. Babylon in its turn was to fall, little more than seventy years later, before the onslaught of the Persian empire. The Persians were followed by the Greeks, and the Greeks by the Romans, and it is of course in Roman times that the events of the New Testament begin to unfold.

It was to Assyria that the northern kingdom of Israel fell, with the sack of Samaria in 722 BC, and to Babylon that the southern kingdom of Judah fell, with the sack of Jerusalem in 587 BC.

Nahum 1:2–8

A charmless chant

An 'opening hymn' considerably fiercer than most modern songs of praise.

Nahum's book as a whole is about Nineveh, but it begins with a section which is all about God. 1:2–8 does not even mention Nineveh, or Nahum, or the troubles of his time. It is timeless truth about God, and it takes the form of a psalm.

Many psalms express human feeling and human experience. But there are many others which are like this one, and describe instead the acts and the character of God. What is more, most of them do as this one does, and concentrate each on a single theme – unlike some modern Christian songs which try to cover too many themes at once and in too little depth.

Nahum's psalm is unlike many of today's songs in another way also. It is fierce. Everything it says about God is true, and can be paralleled elsewhere in the Bible, but there is no mistaking what is put in here and what is left out. Four facts about God are highlighted:

▶ his inexorable justice (verses 2–3a). The slowness of it makes it more, not less, terrible.

▶ his power over his own creation (verses 3b–5) – again, the stern side of the picture: his power not to make, but to unmake.

▶ his wrath against sin, in four frightening nouns: indignation, fierceness, anger, wrath (verse 6).

▶ his impartiality (verses 7–8). If you want a 'beautiful thought' out of Nahum, verse 7 is about the only one you will find, and even that in its context is simply designed to make a contrast – trust the Lord, and be safe; but oppose him, and be sorry.

There is not much charm about this chant. It has nothing of the 'feel-good factor' that we tend to look for in today's songs of praise. But even if we seldom sing of God in these terms, we must at least think of him sometimes like this. His power to destroy is an encouragement when we are aware of the evil around us, and a warning when we remember the evil within us.

Questions

1. In what circumstances might you feel you were outside the 'refuge' (verse 7), and were being made aware of God as the God of verses 2–6?

2. How might today's church become as familiar with biblical psalms, in all their variety, as God's people in Bible times were?

3. What does the Christian gospel have to say to the 'Ninevehs' of today? How would that message relate to Nahum's message in these verses?

Threats and encouragements

A word to God's opponents – but one to his people too.

After Nahum's 'psalm' comes a nine-verse section which is rather different, and presents us with difficulties of three kinds.

▶ There are problems in the original text. If you look at the puzzling Authorized (King James) translation it will give you some inkling of these. Newer translations help to make them clearer.

▶ This section is addressed to 'you', but with two conflicting messages. Is Nahum writing to two distinct 'yous', then? And who are they? (The NIV gives the game away by putting in the names 'Nineveh' and 'Judah' for us, whereas Nahum made his readers think!)

▶ The general truth of 1:2–8 is now applied personally. But since it is being applied to people of Nahum's own time, that makes it harder, not easier, to see how it applies to us.

It is at all events the Lord's deeds and words which Nahum proclaims here. He has threats for one party and encouragements for the other. So we are faced with the real-life facts, the historical events, of Nahum's time. The threats are levelled at Nineveh, and at the Assyrian empire, of which it was the capital (1:1). The encouragement is for Israel (2:2). The northern Israelite kingdom had already been destroyed by the Assyrian invaders, and Judah, the southern kingdom, still lived in dread of them. God speaks, both as impartial judge and as sovereign Lord, to Assyria and Judah in turn.

▶ He tells Assyria what he will do (1:9), how he will do it (1:10), and why (1:11); he tells Judah that this destruction of the enemy will mean deliverance for her (1:12–13).

▶ He repeats the certainty of annihilation for the one (1:14) and of peace for the other (1:15).

▶ He sets the seal on his words by speaking of the future as though it has already happened – the Assyrians may as well abandon hope, for the attacker *'has come'* (2:1, RSV); the Israelites are as good as rescued, 'for the Lord *is restoring . . .'* (2:2, RSV).

Evil will one day be dealt with, the prophets tell us. But they never make light of it. If we say, 'What about the holocaust?', Nahum replies, 'We too had our holocaust, and it was called Assyria'. God allowed it to happen, and that is a great mystery. But the message is that in the end those who perpetrate it are punished and destroyed, and those who suffer are in some way brought through to a secure and prosperous future.

Questions

1. What positive reaction could you imagine to any of these messages? Where there was likely to be a negative reaction, or none at all, what do you think was God's object in sending them?

2. Notice the 'once for all' definiteness of verses 9 and 15. How might we link this with Jesus' words on the cross, 'It is finished' (John 19:30)? How should such scriptures encourage God's people today?
3. Would Nahum have something to say about twentieth-century examples of genocide and mass destruction? If so, what? If not, why not?

Nahum 2:3 – 3:7

'I am against you'

Nahum foresees the destruction of God's great enemies. Once God sets himself against them all hope is lost.

 This section, like the last, poses problems for the translator; the older translations don't go very far towards solving them, but modern ones make the general sense clear.

Nahum is shown a battle scene, or rather a siege. Attacking armies mount an assault on a great city. The defenders abandon their positions and run away like water from a leaking pool. The city is of course Nineveh, and the lion of 2:11–12 stands for Assyria. No longer will it prey on the weaker nations around it.

The words of verse 13 are very important: '"I am against you", declares the LORD Almighty. "I will . . ."'. They are the climax to the description of the battle, and explain it for us. (The same words will appear also in the next chapter, again as the climax to a similar passage.) They tell us half a dozen important things.

▶ The destruction of Nineveh has been described earlier as though it were already happening, but in fact it is still future when Nahum is writing, and it is the Lord who will bring it about. He is behind great historical events of this kind.

▶ He is also able to make them known beforehand through his prophets: this is a prediction.

▶ He is quite prepared to cause, not merely to allow, this sort of destruction.

▶ But when he does so, it is with strict justice, against those who set themselves against him.

▶ Finally, although in these verses the Lord is speaking to the Assyrians, the message as a whole is being given to Nahum to pass on, not to them but to the people of Judah, and for them it is not a warning but an encouragement.

The opening words of 3:5 repeat those of 2:13, so that for the second time the revelation that God gives to Nahum leads up to the words '"I am against you," declares the LORD Almighty. "I will . . ."'

Again Nahum describes the noise and the carnage of battle, but this time three new things are highlighted. God is spelling out for him what is really going on as Nineveh is sacked and the terrible Assyrian empire is brought to its knees.

The sentence of the Judge is revealed (verse 1)

Some new unspecified super-power will mount the attack, but beyond that it is a 'woe', that is, a doom determined and proclaimed by God (3:1). It is like the 'woes' uttered by other prophets (for instance Isaiah 5, Habakkuk 2), by heralds in the book of Revelation (8:13 – 11:15), and by the Lord himself (for example Luke 11:42–52).

The self-centredness of the wicked is revealed (verse 4)

The obvious cause of Assyria's downfall is her cruelty, but beyond that it is her 'wanton lust' and 'witchcraft' (verse 4). Again these are terms which Scripture often uses for those who care nothing for God. They are very apt metaphors for the ways in which people, for their own ends, use and manipulate others, and if necessary discard and destroy them.

The facts of the case are revealed (verses 5–7)

The punishment will certainly be destruction (2:13), but beyond that it is the exposure of the true facts (3:5–7). Nineveh's wilfulness and selfishness will be seen for the disgusting and shameful things they really are.

It is another Old Testament city, Babylon (see pp. 106 and 122), which becomes the ultimate symbol of this determined wilful opposition to God. Unsurprisingly, when the book of Revelation speaks of that city, it is in much the same terms that Nahum uses to speak of this one. We shall find that the parallels between the Old Testament vision and the New Testament one continue through the rest of Nahum 3.

Questions

1. We all fear the shame of exposure (verse 5). How should Christians react to Luke 12:1–3 ('there is nothing concealed that will not be disclosed')?
2. Where might the church perceive, behind the more obvious evils in our world, the kind of motives that verse 4 shows up? God will deal with them in the end, but can anything be done about them now?
3. Is there any modern Nineveh about which Christians could rightly say, with equal conviction (and satisfaction!), that the

Lord is against it? How might the condemnation apply equally to us?

Nahum 3:8–19

Exterminate!

**We can only rejoice when God puts an
end to such an evil thing as Assyria.**

Unlike the previous section, this is from start to finish addressed to 'you', that is to God's enemy. Assyria (the name is at last used in verse 18, for the first and only time in the book) has once and for all decided to oppose the Lord, and must now abide the consequences. As we have seen (p. 106), the Assyrians overran the Middle East, lusting for blood, crying 'Exterminate!' Now the tables are turned, and it is Israel, lusting for revenge, which is crying 'Exterminate!'

The Assyrians know well what happened to the historic city of Thebes, a former capital of Egypt, since it was they who in 663 BC had penetrated deep into Egyptian territory in order to destroy it. And destroyed it was, even though it equalled Nineveh in natural defences, and surpassed it in military resources (verses 8–10). Now they are at the receiving end, and Nineveh will fall just as Thebes fell (verses 11–13). Let it do what it will to defend itself, nothing can save it (verses 14–15). Every kind of leadership fails, the famous super-power is beyond help, and everyone else is delighted at its downfall (verses 16–19).

Well, no doubt everyone *is* delighted. But . . . And what a big 'but' it is! We turn away from our concentrated look into that ancient, barbaric world, and take a deep breath as we find ourselves again in our own modern, civilized world, where surely attitudes are more enlightened? We know that people still suffer as Israelites did at the hands of Assyrians, and we think that is a dreadful thing. But when Assyrians suffer in their turn in the way that Nahum describes, we believe we ought to disapprove of that too, not to revel in it as Nahum does. His spirit of gloating and hatred is quite alien to that of the New Testament, isn't it?

This is one of the great problems of the Bible. It has no simple answer. I have added an attempt at one at the end of this section. But where we *can* range ourselves alongside Nahum is at least in his grim satisfaction that the Lord does in the end put a stop to such gross wickedness as that of the Assyrian beast.

Questions

1. 'Let those who love the LORD hate evil' (Psalm 97:10). What does that mean in practice, in secular society and in the church?
2. There is plenty of evil lurking, usually in disguise, inside every Christian. How eager are we to be rid of it?
3. How can Christians read this book and say, 'this is the word of the LORD, thanks be to God'? (See below.)

The rights and wrongs of hatred

The Lord tells us that hating enemies is wrong (Matthew 5:44), yet other parts of his word seem to contradict this. See, for example, how

- Nahum gloats over the destruction of Nineveh;

- long before, Judges 5:24–31 gloats over the treacherous murder of a Canaanite general;

- long after, Revelation 18 gloats over the ruin of Babylon;

- at the heart of the Bible, Psalm 137:8–9 congratulates the one 'who seizes your infants and dashes them against the rock' –

all apparently with God's approval.

Here is an approach which may help to justify these strange Bible passages. The very object of God's sending his Son into the world was to 'deliver us from evil'. Through Jesus he will one day destroy evil entirely. Through Jesus he is in the meantime rescuing people from its power. But those who *will not* let themselves be detached from evil can't help but be destroyed along with it.

God, of course, knows when people have bound themselves irretrievably to evil, have put themselves beyond redemption, and are ripe for destruction. Old Testament prophecies identify some of them (Joel 3:13; and see Genesis 15:16), and so does the book of Revelation. But for us and our contemporaries, there is no way of telling.

So we are bound:

- to keep working and praying for bad people to be delivered from their evil;

- to rejoice at the destruction of evil in the world around us;

- to be equally eager for the doing away of evil that we cherish in our own hearts.

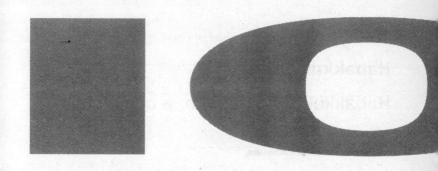

HABAKKUK THE QUESTIONER

Habakkuk 1:1 – 3:19

Habakkuk 1:1–4

Habakkuk's first psalm: a complaint

**Do you complain that God is doing nothing?
Then one thing at least he's doing, and
that is moving you to complain!**

As with Nahum, God's message through
Habakkuk is called an 'oracle' (verse 1) or
'burden'. 'Burden' is a very apt word. Any
prophecy is a heavy responsibility which
God places on his servant the prophet, to be carried and then
delivered to those for whom it is intended.

Habakkuk's burden turns out (verse 2) to be a complaint. (He
is inspired *by* God to complain *about* God! More on that at the
end of this section.) This sort of cry to God is unusual in the
prophets, but frequent in the Psalms – Psalm 13 is one of the
closest parallels. We may remember that Micah 7 and Nahum 1
also contained psalms, though psalms of a different kind.
Habakkuk may in fact be taken to be a sequence of three psalms,
each beginning with the cry 'O LORD' and the third of them even
having a typical psalm-like heading and tailpiece (3:1, 19), with
two responses from God in between.

This first one complains about a whole bunch of wrongs
(verse 3) which the Lord seems to be ignoring. If he is a holy
God, surely he ought not to turn a blind eye to such things?

Why is he doing nothing to put them right, and to punish the wrongdoers?

It would be a help to know the particular situation Habakkuk had in mind, and we are given some clues (verse 4). The evils he speaks of have to do with a breakdown in 'the law', that is the Torah, God's own law given to Israel to set her apart from all other nations. So it is the Israelite community that has gone wrong. 'The wicked' and 'the righteous' are those of God's people who have thrown over God's law and those who are still trying to keep it, and the former seem to be gaining control. Many believers since Habakkuk's time will have echoed his dismay, both over the wrongs they see among God's people and over the fact that God seems not to care.

Questions

1. When wrong things happen, have you ever tried complaining to God (as well as, or instead of, to the newspapers or to the authorities)? What was the result?
2. Our world is no stranger to situations where 'conflict abounds' so that 'the law is paralysed' – that is, the forces of disorder are stronger than the forces of order. What kinds of solution are put forward, and how should Christians regard them?
3. How and where do similar situations arise among God's people?

'57 varieties' of prophecy

The 'burdens' God laid on his prophets were of many different kinds. The classic kind was prediction (Deuteronomy 18:21f). But God was just as likely to send a message about the present as about the future. Indeed his prophets might not necessarily bring a challenge about the present, but simply a comment on it, or even nothing more than an account of it, as we have seen in Joel.

When Nahum expresses fierce approval of God's punishing of the wicked, even that human reaction is prophecy. And here Habakkuk takes the process one step further still – he sees God apparently *not* punishing the wicked, and complains that God must be wrong, and that very complaint is part of the prophetic message God has given him!

We have a great God. His plans have taken into account the sins as well as the obediences of humanity, and they reckon with the doubts and accusations of his people as well as with their prayers and praises. Whatever unlikely facts or feelings we find expressed in Scripture, in all of them God is saying, 'Listen to this: I am speaking to you through it'.

Habakkuk 1:5–11

The Lord's first answer

We may find our complaints dealt with in the unlikeliest way we could imagine.

We may have been surprised how varied are the voices through which God speaks in Scripture (see *'57 varieties' of prophecy*). Habakkuk himself will be surprised how varied are the means through which God acts in history (verses 5–11). 'You will not believe this', says God; and he goes on to describe, to the prophet's shocked and incredulous dismay, how he intends to deal with the situation Habakkuk is complaining about – a proliferation of great wrongs among his own people.

Habakkuk had probably thought what we would have thought.

▶ God might have prevented bad influences from creeping in in the first place.

▶ If they had crept in, he might have enabled all sensible folk to see them for what they were, and reject them.

▶ If they did get established he might somehow have nullified their effects, or raised up strong leaders to combat them.

▶ The righteous might have overcome the wicked, or the wicked might simply in some miraculous way have been removed.

God might have done, and sometimes has done, any of these things.

But in this case he did none of them. Instead, he pointed away from his people altogether, to 'the nations' (verse 5), the secular world around them. There he would mobilize ruthless forces (verse 6), with values and standards which owed nothing to him (verse 7). 'From afar', far beyond the boundaries of his people's familiar religious world (verse 8), he would bring this onslaught, to punish them (verses 9–10) by means of secular powers which had 'gods' of their own, and no idea that they were merely tools in the hands of the God of Israel (verse 11).

This was God's answer to Habakkuk's complaint that he seemed to be doing nothing. It is a sobering thought that the same God is still at work behind the power politics of today's world.

Questions

1. How can you find the proper balance between credulity (believing uncritically almost anything anyone says) and lack of faith (unwillingness to believe even what God says)?
2. In how much detail do you think God controls the doings of modern secular governments? In what ways do you think he is at work in situations known to you?
3. What were the features of the rise of Babylon, as these verses describe it, which God said Habakkuk 'would not believe'? What similar things does God do today which Christians find amazingly unlikely?

Babylon

The Babylonians (this is the NIV's substitute for 'Chaldeans', the term which Habakkuk used) were the last great enemy of Israel in Old Testament history. Their capital city, Babylon, or Babel, figures throughout the Bible from Genesis to Revelation, and is both an actual place and a symbol. It symbolizes human society trying to live independently of God.

Babylonia twice became a great power in the ancient world. Round about 2000 BC the first Babylonian empire flourished, in the area we should call Southern Iraq. Many of the events of the book of Genesis, especially those connected with Abraham and his family, date from around this time. The rise of the second or Neo-Babylonian empire, after centuries of decline, is the one that Habakkuk foresees. Babylonian armies destroyed the Assyrian capital, Nineveh, in 612 BC, the event which Nahum predicted with such relish. But they went on to attack Judah also, and it is that prospect which is going to fill Habakkuk with dismay.

Habakkuk 1:12-17

Habakkuk's second psalm:
another complaint

If God *is* doing something, why doesn't he do it more quickly?

The second of Habakkuk's psalms begins, like the other two, by calling on the Lord. He has found that the Lord's ear will hear any prayer, even one full of doubts and com-  plainings, and that his hand will use any tool, even the secular powers of this world. The prophet knows too that there are other great truths wrapped up in the very name 'LORD', and verse 12 unwraps some of them.

- 'LORD' is God's special name, to be used by those he binds to himself by covenant, and Habakkuk rightly sees that he can therefore call the LORD 'my God'.

- He also reasons that since this God is eternal, those who belong to him cannot die; God may punish Judah by means of the Babylonians, but he will not destroy it.

For all that, Habakkuk still has questions. To him, even wicked Israelites are 'more righteous' than wicked Babylonians, so how can a God who hates evil use such evil forces, and leave their victims as helpless as a shoal of fish caught in a great net? It's not as though the 'fishermen' recognize who has set the whole thing up – they reckon the catch is due to their own fishing skills!

What was it that really bothered Habakkuk? It was not so much 'the problem of evil' in itself – the question why, in a world and in a church which both belong to God, and in which he is constantly at work, there is evil at all. Rather, Habakkuk was asking questions about *time*. '*How long*' will God let Israelite wickedness go on? asks his first psalm (verse 2). Is Babylonian wickedness going to '*keep on*' destroying the nations? asks his second psalm (verse 17). Why doesn't God nip these things in the bud? Have they not gone on long enough?

These are practical questions we can sympathize with. Why evil is here, and how it got here, are deep theological problems. The fact is that it *is* here, and Habakkuk is asking why God doesn't do something about it sooner rather than later.

We await an answer!

Questions

1. For what New Testament reasons can Christians agree with Habakkuk, 'We will not die'?
2. How would you answer Habakkuk's question about God's slowness?
3. In what way might a secular power today 'sacrifice to its net' (verse 16)?

Eternal life – an Old Testament promise

Eternal life is not something which we know about from the New Testament only, and of which the Old Testament says nothing. There is a hint of it in this passage, for example.

When Habakkuk says 'Are you not from everlasting? We will not die', he is speaking in the first instance of the survival of the nation. But the principle goes much deeper, whether or not such deeper truth was in his mind. For Jesus makes a similar connection when he is teaching about the resurrection of the dead (Mark 12:26–27). When God says to Moses 'I am the God of Abraham, Isaac, and Jacob', those three men have long since been dead. But if in Moses' time God is alive, and is their God, then they too must be alive in him. The same is true of every believer, whether in Old Testament or in New Testament times – all who have been drawn to the living God and have become one with him. As Jesus says elsewhere, 'Because I live, you also will live' (John 14:19).

Habakkuk 2:1–5

The background to the Lord's second answer

Be reassured – God's people are *not* on the verge of extinction, and their enemies are *not* unstoppable. The reason? What one has and the other lacks is *faith*.

Conjunctions matter! Take for example the two little sentences, 'I spoke. He didn't', and the four little words 'and', 'but', 'so', and 'because'. You could join together the two sentences with any one of the four conjunctions, and get four quite different ideas of what was going on. (One of the marks of a good translation of the Bible, by the way, is its carefulness about conjunctions. Good theology depends on them.)

Habakkuk 2:1–5 is a kind of conjunction on a large scale. It links what has gone before with the Lord's second formal response and Habakkuk's third and last psalm, and helps to explain the whole thing. It is as though the rest of the book were a dialogue declaimed on stage, while these five verses were a brief conversation between the two actors behind the scenes half way through.

Habakkuk's questions are real questions. His object is not to discuss religion, still less to score points off an opponent. He is going up to the 'ramparts', or watch-tower – as we might say, he is 'on the look-out' for answers. He is eager to hear whatever the Lord has to say.

In the Lord's reply, he is told that he had grasped the nub of the matter when he couched his question in terms of *time*: 'How long?' (1:2). The Lord explains that:

▶ answers will be revealed at the 'appointed time', that is, that he decides when;

▶ it may seem long delayed;

▶ it is nonetheless certain, so Habakkuk must be patient.

On the other hand, although the content of the message is that things will be made plain only in God's good time, that message itself is for now. The Lord wants Habakkuk to write it down (on tablets of clay or stone: such inscriptions have lasted to this day from the world of Bible times); not, as verse 3 is sometimes taken to mean, 'so that whoever runs may read it', i.e. clearly, but 'so that whoever reads it may run with it' (NIV margin), i.e. challengingly.

The message is, in a nutshell, 'the righteous will live by his faith'. Unlike the person described in the rest of verses 4–5, the one who is right with God is the one who will survive, and that will be because he continues to trust God, against all appearances, and through any amount of delay.

Questions

1. It is said that God always answers prayers with 'yes', 'no' or 'wait'. When you ask God hard questions, how long are you prepared to wait for answers? And are you willing to accept them when they do come? How do you recognize an answer to prayer? Think of examples.
2. Compare verse 4 with the three New Testament quotations of it mentioned in the note below, and discuss how each passage explains faith and its results.
3. What methods of publicizing God's message seem most effective in making the reader (or hearer) 'run with it'?

'The righteous will live by his faith'

The New Testament finds a key spiritual principle in Habakkuk 2:4. There is true righteousness and true life only where there is true faith. Paul's point in Romans 1:17 and Galatians 3:11, where he quotes this verse, is that to those in whom God finds faith he gives righteousness and life. Hebrews 10:37–39 takes faith in the sense of faithfulness. But the two senses of the word are inseparable. Faith means that I trust God, faithfulness means that he can trust me. You can't have either without the other.

Habakkuk 2:6–20

The Lord's second answer

Are you baffled by God's use of Babylonian wickedness to punish his own people? Well, wickedness it remains, and it will itself be punished in its turn.

Now comes the Lord's formal response to Habakkuk's second psalm of complaint. First the prophet had asked how long the Lord would ignore the wickedness of Judah, and  the Lord replied that he was mobilizing the Babylonians to punish it. So then Habakkuk asked how long the Lord would ignore the wickedness of the Babylonians, which was even worse.

The Lord's reply now is in the form of five 'woes' in which he pronounces the Babylonians' doom.

They are greedy: so they will suffer at the hands of the very people they have robbed (verses 6–8). They will be like burglars finding that on the second visit the householder is awake, the alarm is set, and the dogs will bite.

They are complacent: so their security will be undermined (verses 9–11). The very stones and timbers of the great structures they have built will rebel against them.

They have sought notoriety, founding cities to perpetuate their name (verses 12–14). So they are doomed to be forgotten; a day is coming when the renown of God's name only will fill the world.

They are crude and heartless, and care nothing about putting others in shameful situations (verses 15–17). So they in turn will be shamed and scorned.

They are idolatrous, for all kinds of other gods take the place of the true God in their lives (verses 18–20). And what a noise they make in the worship of those gods! So they will one day have to recognize that 'the LORD is in his holy temple', and that 'all the earth' will have to 'be silent before him'.

Five times over, then, God promises that he will not turn a blind eye to the wickedness of the Babylonians. Not only will he punish it, but he will repeatedly make the punishment fit the crime. In doing so he gives us a glimpse into one of the great mysteries of biblical theology. For the harsh treatment the Babylonians have in store for Judah is both ordained by God as a just punishment for Judah's sin, and at the same time deliberate wickedness on the Babylonians' part, for which they themselves will be punished.

Questions

1. It is easy to regard the five evils listed here as other people's sins. Are you aware of the beginnings of any of them in your own heart? Identify them and consider how they should be dealt with.
2. The ancient 'eye for an eye, tooth for a tooth' principle was simply the rule of letting the punishment fit the crime. Can you think of examples, in Bible times or since, where crimes or sins have been dealt with in this way?
3. How might a church fellowship profit from a series of studies on these 'woes', addressed as they are to the enemies of God's people?

129

Habakkuk 3:1–19

Habakkuk's final psalm

Habakkuk's God is the God who accomplished great things in the famous days of old. Whatever the appearances, we may be sure he is in the process of doing the same today.

In chapter 3 Habakkuk the poet surpasses himself. He produces a psalm worthy to stand alongside any of David's. He even adds, in verses 1 and 19b, directions as to how it is to be performed.

The opening and closing verses of the psalm proper (2 and 19a) express the heart of his message, and enclose three paragraphs or stanzas between them. Why he begins with the memorable words of verse 2, especially the prayer which in the old versions runs 'Revive thy work in the midst of the years', will become clear as we go on.

The God of then (verses 3–7)

The next five verses account for the awe at God's name that Habakkuk has just spoken of. They are a description in vivid picture language of some of the unforgettable events of the exodus and the conquest, the time when God brought his people Israel out of slavery in Egypt and into the promised land of Canaan.

The God of now (verses 8–15)

At verse 8 there is a change. Habakkuk's theme is still the days of Moses and Joshua, but instead of speaking *about* God, he now begins to speak *to* him. Now, in Habakkuk's time, the God of the exodus is still alive and active. The prophet is reminding him: 'It was you who did all those great things'. Hence his plea at the outset, 'Revive thy work in the midst of the years' – renew it, do again now the kind of thing you did then. That was a time when your people saw both your wrath and your mercy; we need to see both of them again now – your wrath against the wicked, and your mercy towards the repentant.

The God of me (verses 16–18)

These closing verses are Habakkuk's own confession of faith. He is all too aware of the wrath, but is now trusting that in God's good time he will see the mercy too.

A version of verses 17–18 is still to be found in some of our hymnbooks:

Though vine nor fig-tree neither
   Their wonted fruit should bear,
Though all the fields should wither,
   Nor flocks nor herds be there,
Yet, God the same abiding,
   His praise shall tune my voice;
For while in him confiding,
   I cannot but rejoice.

William Cowper, who wrote that hymn ('Sometimes a light surprises The Christian while he sings'), suffered from terrible depression, and could sympathize more than most with

Habakkuk's questionings. The hymn-writer and the prophet learned, as many others have learned, both to be urgent in asking and to be patient and confident in waiting for answers.

Questions

1. In what practical ways can the church when it meets remind itself of God's great doings in the past?
2. In what sense should we expect the Lord to 'renew them in our day' (verse 2)?
3. How does the confidence of verses 17–18 relate to such shortages in the modern world?

ZEPHANIAH
THE SEER

Zephaniah 1:1 – 3:20

Zephaniah 1:1–7

High drama

**This far-reaching message of 'the LORD's day'
brings together the fate of the world
and the state of the church.**

The way Zephaniah's little book begins
ought to arrest our attention. He seems to be
quite a special person, and so does the one to
whom he is speaking.

The prophet is noteworthy

When the Bible tells us a man's name, it often tells us also
whose son he was. It is a custom that in English has given
us many surnames (John Johnson, for example), and in some
other languages still does. But Zephaniah is the only prophet
whose 'surnames' go right back to his great-grandfather's
generation, and they appear to show that he was descended
from no less a person than the great king Hezekiah. What
is more, all but one of the names in his family tree include
the name of Israel's God 'Yah' (the LORD), so we may take
it that he came from a God-fearing background as well as
a royal one.

The king is noteworthy

We may also take it that Josiah was not simply the king who happened to be reigning when Zephaniah prophesied, but a willing listener to his words. He too was a special person, outstanding among the kings of Judah for his desire to love and serve God.

We are given a detailed picture of the man and his times in 2 Kings 22–23 and 2 Chronicles 34–35. Josiah had to cope with great difficulties in his home background, in his kingdom at large, and on the international scene. Yet as the Chronicles account tells us he 'did what was right in the eyes of the LORD', having as a teenager begun 'to seek the God of his father David'. He has gone down in history as a great and godly man.

The message is noteworthy

With such distinguished people involved, the message that is being spoken and heard has a fierceness that comes as something of a shock. The Lord threatens a fearful destruction. He will sweep away (verses 2–3) all he brought into being on the last two days of creation (Genesis 1:20–31). Perhaps he means the sweeping not of a broom but of a sword, which he then thrusts straight at his own people (verses 4–6) to cut off those among them who call themselves by his name yet care nothing for him.

So the punishment of the earth's population in general is closely connected with the sin of God's people in particular. What a sobering thought for well-meaning believers like Josiah – and us!

And another sobering thought is here in verse 7, and will come back several times in Zephaniah. Christians tend to use the words 'the Lord's day' to mean Sunday – 'O day of rest and gladness, O day of joy and light', as an old hymn put it. But Zephaniah will talk repeatedly about 'a day of distress and anguish, a day of trouble and ruin' (1:15). That is what *he* means by 'the Lord's day'. Most English translations call it 'the day of the LORD', but of course the two phrases are only different ways of saying exactly the same thing.

Zechariah's preoccupation with the 'Lord's day/day of the LORD', in its doom-laden sense, not its happy 'Sunday' sense, brings us full circle. He, the last of our six prophets, is taking up a theme which equally dominated the message of Joel, the first of them, and appears in others besides.

Questions

1. How might these verses make a sincere believer like Josiah (or you!) personally uncomfortable?
2. Some Israelites who worshipped Baal or Molech would have said that this was quite compatible with the faith of Israel, or even 'another aspect of its rich diversity'. What 'foreign gods' do you think may infiltrate today's church?
3. What do you think is the connection between God's global threat (verses 2–3) and his threat to his own people (verses 4–7)?

Zephaniah 1:8–13

An immediate Lord's day

In case we miss the impact of 'The day of the LORD is near', we should remind ourselves that 'near' can mean both 'at *this time*' and 'in *this place*'.

Zephaniah's 'day of the LORD', like the traditional Christian 'Lord's day', is a religious occasion. In Old Testament times this would have involved 'a sacrifice', as 1:7 has told us. But instead of the usual sacrificial animals it is people that he has 'consecrated' for slaughter. They are the wicked, who the first part of the chapter says are to be swept away and cut off (verses 2–3), and more particularly wicked people in God's own city (verses 4–6).

Verses 8–13 spell out the latter point, the particular one. 'The day of the LORD', which is 'the day of the LORD's sacrifice', may be nearer than they think, both in time and space.

▶ It could be soon, it could be now, that God will deal with his opponents. They are those among his people who for all their good opinion of themselves show by their lifestyle and the way they think and act that they are not right with him. The time could be this time.

137

And that was in fact how it happened. It literally was 'the king's sons' who were punished. Three of Josiah's sons followed him on the throne of Judah, all broke faith with their father and his God, and each in turn lost his crown.

► In the same way, 'the day of the LORD' could arrive right here – at the Fish Gate, in the New Quarter, districts of Jerusalem which Zephaniah's hearers know well. And that too was how it actually happened. People living up on the hill or working down in the market were to see enemy armies invading their own streets. They learned the hard way that 'the day of the LORD' would happen not in the remote future, but now; not somewhere else, but here.

Some Christians still think of the Lord's day as an event which comes round once every week. We really need to be prepared for it to arrive even sooner than next Sunday! Suppose the Lord were to come into our lives to 'search . . . with lamps' (verse 12) this very day? Is there anything at all that that search might reveal, about which we should dare to say 'Oh, the Lord wouldn't care one way or the other about that'?

Questions

1. Pinpoint areas of your life about which you have tended to say, 'The Lord will do nothing, either good or bad' (verse 12).
2. Suggest some of the less obvious ways in which a church may become punishably complacent.
3. Bad things happening to people like ourselves, in societies like our own, shake us out of complacency in a way that remote disasters don't. What positive lessons can we learn from these nearer events?

Who are the culprits?

It is not quite clear who is in mind in 1:8–9. In verse 8 'princes' and 'king's sons' may mean Israelite rulers in general, but on the other hand they may mean specifically the sons of King Josiah. As we have seen, none of them followed in his father's footsteps. Three of them, as well as one of Josiah's grandsons, reigned after him, and all were deposed from the throne in quick succession, one of them being the last king ever to reign over Judah; their sins were the last straw, and brought about the final destruction of Jerusalem by the Babylonian king Nebuchadnezzar.

'Foreign clothes' may have something to do with non-Israelite religions, and robes worn in their religious ceremonies.

To 'avoid stepping on the threshold' (if that is a correct translation) may be connected with the events described in 1 Samuel 5:1–5, when the Philistines had captured and put in the temple of their god Dagon the sacred ark of the God of Israel. The following morning they had found Dagon's statue fallen down before it, broken to pieces in the doorway; from then on, 'stepping on the threshold' was forbidden among the Philistines, and the superstition had perhaps spread to Israel.

At all events, everyone mentioned in these two verses is, for whatever reason, deserving of the Lord's punishment.

Zephaniah 1:14–18

An ultimate Lord's day

Even if fearsome 'Lord's day' events happen here and now, we must not imagine that there is not also a final one looming ahead for the whole world.

If we had lived in the reign of Josiah and heard the prophecy of Zephaniah, and had then stayed on in Jerusalem for another twenty years or so after Josiah's death, the  words of 1:8–13 would have come true before our eyes. Threats of foreign invasion would have become reality, and we should have witnessed the Lord's punishment of his people as we saw Jerusalem destroyed by Babylonian armies.

If we had then recalled how God's message through Zephaniah continued in the last part of chapter 1, we might have assumed to begin with that verse 14 too was talking about what would happen 'on that day'. But if that were so, then in this next paragraph the prophet really would be laying it on thick! He gradually opens up before us something far more dreadful even than the destruction of God's holy city Jerusalem. By the end of the chapter, 'the great day of the LORD . . . near and coming quickly' (verse 14) turns out to be the day when God destroys 'the whole world' and 'all who live in the earth' (verse 18).

The prophecy began in the same way, with the Lord threatening to sweep away every living thing from the face of the earth (1:2–3), and thus to undo what he did on the fifth and sixth days of creation. So perhaps the same thing is in mind also when six times over in verses 15 and 16 'that day' is described as 'a day of' some great evil. Roman Catholics have long known verse 15 in the form of the Latin words in the Requiem Mass which speak of the end of the world – *Dies irae, dies illa*, 'The day of wrath, that dreadful day'. The devastation the Lord's day will bring will put into reverse the whole work of creation as the first chapter of Genesis describes it.

So is Zephaniah confused, as many people are, on the subject of what the future holds? Did he think that the destruction of Jerusalem would be the end of the world, and discover in the event that it wasn't?

No, it is not a case of the final Lord's day being scheduled for one date rather than another. We should think of it as an event which is always 'waiting in the wings'. It has already come on to the scene many times in history. We have to be prepared at any time for its final, overwhelming appearance.

Questions

1. Is it realistic, or even possible, to think of God in our own personal prayer times as one who brings 'distress and anguish'? ('Dear Father, I know you're quite capable of doing dreadful things . . .') How can we ensure that we keep a proper balance between our view of God as loving Saviour and destroying judge?

2. In the Old Testament, 'the people' (verse 17) usually means God's people, but here it is a different word and means simply 'people', the human race. How can they all 'have sinned against the LORD', when many of them have never heard of him?

141

3. If verse 18a ('Neither their silver nor their gold will be able to save them') is part of the church's message to the world, how is it to be proclaimed?

A clear view of the future?

Zephaniah may or may not have realized that his message was about two separate comings of the day of the LORD, one within a few years and the other at the end of history. Such things were not always made clear to the prophets (1 Peter 1:10–12). As we have already noted in considering the prophecy of Joel (see p. 46), they often saw the future like a view of mountains – you might not be able to tell whether all the peaks belonged to the same range, or whether some were much more remote than others.

Jesus recognized the difficulty when he explained that another destruction of Jerusalem, which some of his disciples would see, would still not be the final 'day of the LORD' when he himself would return (Matthew 24:15–28).

Zephaniah 2:1–15

A warning to everyone

There are divine warnings both for the church and for the world. Each ought to be aware of God's dealings with the other.

What a mixed-up, contradictory thing the church of Jesus Christ is! So far as we are concerned, this is what Zephaniah's second chapter is about. For the church simply means the people of God, whether they are a nation (as they are for so much of Old Testament history) or an international fellowship (as they have been ever since). The kind of thing Zephaniah says to the church of his own time he is also saying to the church of our time.

The first three verses of the chapter are addressed directly to God's 'Israel', his church. And as I say, what a mixed bunch we are!

▶ On the one hand (verses 1–2) God is speaking to a 'nation', and that is a word normally used for the pagan nations, not Israel. 'You are as bad as the rest,' he is saying.

▶ On the other hand (verse 3), within the 'shameful nation' there are still to be found the 'humble of the land . . . who do what he commands'.

But both 'shameful' and 'humble' need to be reminded that the final Lord's day will be the day of the Lord's anger.

God speaks to the surrounding peoples (verses 4–15)

(See the map on p. 18.) He does not shut his eyes to what is going on outside the church, though each of his judgments on the secular world around is in some way related to his own people.

▶ **Philistia and Canaan** (verses 4–7) were originally the nations in the centre and west of the Promised Land. They were non-Semitic peoples who, because of their wickedness, should have been driven out long before, and their land should have been occupied by Israel. They will indeed come to nothing, and what was theirs will indeed be taken over by God's people.

▶ **Moab and Ammon** (verses 8–11) lay east of the land. They were Semites, related to Israel (see Genesis 19); their ancestor Lot was Abraham's nephew and worshipped Abraham's God. They too will be destroyed and dispossessed, in their case 'for insulting and mocking the people of the Lord Almighty'. Unlike the Philistines and the Canaanites, they should have known better.

▶ **Egypt** (which is probably what 'Cushites' means) **and Assyria** (verses 12–15) represented the super-powers of the ancient world, one away to the south-west, the other to the north-east. They generally considered God's people beneath their notice: 'I am, and there is none besides me', was their arrogant attitude.

God intends his own people to overhear

Taking his words to these six nations out of their context, Israel might well have said complacently, 'Serve them right'. But in the context, we realize what God is really telling his people: 'When l give notice of the coming day of wrath to people who *don't* pretend to know me, how much more should my warnings be heeded by people who *do* claim to know me!'

Questions

1. Does the 'perhaps' of verse 3 shake your confidence in God? If not, why not?
2. How can a church know when God is addressing it as 'Shameful nation', and when as 'You humble of the land'?
3. Should we expect in today's world judgments from God equivalent to those in this chapter? If so, where and how might they fall?

Zephaniah 3:1–8

Two agendas in Jerusalem

There are conflicting forces within God's community. The Lord is still there, but so are self-centredness and arrogance.

God has been passing sentence on the nations which are Judah's neighbours – Philistia and Canaan, Moab and Ammon, Cush (Egypt?) and Assyria. Towards the end of chapter 2, along with the destruction of Assyria he speaks of the devastation of its capital city Nineveh. Assyria was the object of Nahum's denunciations too, and he regularly addressed it as 'Nineveh'. Zephaniah calls it 'the carefree city that lived in safety' (2:15).

Perhaps he guesses that his Israelite readers, relieved at having the spotlight of 2:1–3 turned away from them, are settling back again to enjoy the discomfiture of the 'carefree city'. So, leading them on, he declares in the very next verse (3:1), 'Woe to the city of oppressors, rebellious and defiled!' 'Hear, hear,' they all cry. 'She obeys no-one, she accepts no correction,' he says. 'Yes, yes,' they rejoin – and then realize he is not now talking about Nineveh at all, but about a city that knows the Lord (though she doesn't trust him), and that keeps aloof from one who is nevertheless '*her* God'. It is Jerusalem, not Nineveh, he is lashing; it is his hearers themselves, the city and people of God, or in our terms the church.

Two attitudes

There are two attitudes in Jerusalem (verses 3–5), two opposite attitudes.

➤ Here are the people who matter, or who think they do: officials and rulers, prophets and priests. What is their attitude? They are self-centred, greedy, arrogant, unspiritual people.

➤ Here is the one who really matters: the Lord is still in Jerusalem, keeping things on an even keel, ensuring that right is not altogether forgotten.

This is how the church has so often been, in Old Testament times and New. The life of the individual believer is all too likely to follow the same pattern.

Two agendas

There are two agendas in Jerusalem (verses 6–7), two conflicting agendas.

▶ The Lord is reminding his people how he deals with wickedness. They have witnessed it in the way he has brought down the nations of 2:4–15: 'Their cities are destroyed' (verse 6). So he speaks to them directly, as he did in 2:1–3: he says 'to *the* city, "Surely you will fear me and accept correction!"' (verse 7a).

▶ The leaders are determined to follow their own agenda all the same (verse 7b).

This too is what happens in the life of the church (and in the life of the Christian). As Galatians 5:17 puts it, the sinful nature and the Spirit of God are in conflict with each other.

But take warning. When the Lord comes 'to assemble the nations', *all* who go their own sinful way – even if they think of themselves as real Jerusalem people – will come under the fire of God's fierce anger (verse 8).

Questions

1. How would you have reacted to verses 1–4, if you had been King Josiah, doing your best to bring about reforms?
2. How and why might the Lord nowadays set before the church warnings like those of verses 6–7?

Zephaniah 3:9–20

Beyond the burning

After the final day of the Lord has dealt with everything evil, it will usher in a new world.

You may have noticed that the Lord's day has figured in each of the sections into which we have divided Zephaniah so far.

- 'The day of the LORD' (1:7)

- 'The day of the LORD's sacrifice' (1:8)

- 'The great day of the LORD' (1:14)

- 'The day of the LORD's wrath/anger' (2:2–3)

- 'The day I will stand up to testify' (3:8)

By 3:8, if not before, the Lord's day Zephaniah is talking about is the final Lord's day, when 'the whole world' will be burned up. That climax must surely be the end?

But no. With 3:9 we come out beyond the burning into another world, which gives a whole new look to the meaning of the Lord's day. 'On that day,' 'at that time,' says Zephaniah repeatedly, you will find that the day of wrath turns out to be a day not only of unmaking but of remaking.

'Come and see the shining hope that Christ's apostle saw,' says a modern song based on verses from the Book of Revelation. There at the climax of the New Testament we find the very same thing that we have here:

> If anyone's name was not found written in the book of life, he was thrown into the lake of fire.
>
> Then I saw a new heaven and a new earth ... I saw the Holy City, the new Jerusalem, coming down out of heaven from God, prepared as a bride beautifully dressed for her husband. And I heard a loud voice from the throne saying, 'Now the dwelling of God is with men, and he will live with them. They will be his people, and God himself will be with them and be their God. He will wipe every tear from their eyes. There will be no more death or mourning or crying or pain, for the old order of things has passed away'.
>
> (Revelation 20:15 – 21:4)

As Zephaniah relays what he hears, and describes what he sees, it ought not to surprise us that his words tally with what other parts of the Bible promise to God's people on that great day:

- ▶ Their speech will no longer be unworthy, at cross purposes, liable to misunderstanding – they will find themselves all 'talking the same language', united in the service of God (verse 9);

- ▶ The separated will be reunited (verse 10);

- ▶ There will be no more pride, sin, deceit, or fear (verses 11–13);

- ▶ There will be no more punishment, oppression, or suffering (verses 14–15);

- ▶ There will instead be the joy of the Lord's own immediate presence (verses 16–17);

- ▶ The church itself will be praised and honoured – just like

149

the glorious bride of Christ in the verses just quoted from Revelation 21 (verses 18–20). Indeed that chapter is the New Testament counterpart of this one in all sorts of ways.

God's picture of the new world which that day will usher in is passed on by Zephaniah in terms of the world he knows: it is 'this city', the 'holy hill', Zion and Jerusalem. But it is so perfect and so permanent that we realize this is heaven we are being shown.

Questions

1. How *desirable* is the next world to you? Would you rather be there than here? If not, in what ways could these verses change your mind?
2. What, according to this passage, will heaven mean to the church (as distinct from the individual believer)? How might that colour what the church thinks important in this world?
3. Do these verses imply that there could be a wonderful new civilization emerging after a nuclear holocaust? How can we distinguish between what is meant pictorially and what is literal in this prophecy?

For further reading

David W. Baker, *Nahum, Habakkuk, Zephaniah, Tyndale Old Testament Commentary* (IVP, 1988)

David W. Baker, T. Desmond Alexander and Bruce K. Waltke, *Obadiah, Jonah, Micah, Tyndale Old Testament Commentary* (IVP, 1988)

Peter C. Craigie, *The Twelve Prophets, The Daily Study Bible* (2 vols, St Andrews Press 1984/1985)

Martin Goldsmith, *Habakkuk and Joel: God is Sovereign in History* (Marshalls, 1982)

David Allan Hubbard, *Joel and Amos, Tyndale Old Testament Commentary* (IVP, 1989)